Create Microsoft®

Check the Web for Updates

To check for updates or corrections relevant to this book and/or CD-ROM visit our updates page on the Web at **http://www.prima-tech.com/support/**.

Send Us Your Comments

To comment on this book or any other PRIMA TECH title, visit our reader response page on the Web at **http://www.prima-tech.com/comments**.

How to Order

For information on quantity discounts, contact the publisher: Prima Publishing, P.O. Box 1260BK, Rocklin, CA 95677-1260; (916) 787-7000. On your letterhead, include information concerning the intended use of the books and the number of books you want to purchase. For individual orders, turn to the back of this book for more information.

Create Microsoft® PowerPoint® 2002 Presentations

NANCY STEVENSON

A DIVISION OF PRIMA PUBLISHING

A Division of Prima Publishing

Prima Publishing and colophon are registered trademarks of Prima Communications, Inc. PRIMA TECH and *In a Weekend* are registered trademarks of Prima Communications, Inc., Roseville, California 95661.

Publisher: Stacy L. Hiquet
Managing Editor: Sandy Doell
Associate Marketing Manager: Jennifer Breece
Acquisitions Editor: Debbie Abshier
Project Editor: Heather Talbot
Technical Reviewer: Brian Reilly
Copy Editor: Kris Simmons
Interior Layout: Jill Flores
Cover Design: Prima Design Team
CD-ROM Producer: Jason Haines
Indexer: Sharon Shock
Proofreader: Mitzi Foster

Microsoft and PowerPoint are registered trademarks of Microsoft Corporation in the United States and/or other countries.

All other trademarks are the property of their respective owners.

Important: Prima Publishing cannot provide software support. Please contact the appropriate software manufacturer's technical support line or Web site for assistance.

Prima Publishing and the author have attempted throughout this book to distinguish proprietary trademarks from descriptive terms by following the capitalization style used by the manufacturer.

Information contained in this book has been obtained by Prima Publishing from sources believed to be reliable. However, because of the possibility of human or mechanical error by our sources, Prima Publishing, or others, the Publisher does not guarantee the accuracy, adequacy, or completeness of any information and is not responsible for any errors or omissions or the results obtained from use of such information. Readers should be particularly aware of the fact that the Internet is an ever-changing entity. Some facts may have changed since this book went to press.

ISBN: 0-7615-3397-4
Library of Congress Catalog Card Number: 2001-086683
Printed in the United States of America
00 01 02 03 04 DD 10 9 8 7 6 5 4 3 2 1

To Bryn and Dylan, who bring humor and fun into my busy writing days.

ACKNOWLEDGMENTS

Many thanks to Heather Talbot for her able handling of the editorial aspects of this book. Thanks also to Prima and Debbie Abshier, a terrific acquisitions editor, for giving me the opportunity to write it, and to Brian Reilly for his technical edit.

ABOUT THE AUTHOR

Nancy Stevenson is a professional author and consultant with more than two dozen books to her credit, on topics ranging from computer technology to e-commerce. She has also written articles for several national magazines. Nancy holds a Certificate in Distance Learning Design from the University of Washington. She has honed her skills with PowerPoint presentation design in her work in the corporate world in the software and publishing industries, and as a consultant.

CONTENTS

APPENDIX B
Ten Steps to an Effective Web Presentation 213

APPENDIX C
Online Resource Directory 231

Appendix D
Talk the Talk with Speech Recognition. 239

INTRODUCTION

They say that good things come to those who wait, but I say, why wait? The premise of this book is instant gratification: You need to learn your way around PowerPoint and get a presentation done, and you don't have weeks to do it. By sitting down for several hours a day over one weekend (not even a three-day weekend!), you can create your first PowerPoint 2002 presentation. Along the way, you're going to pick up all the basic skills you need to use PowerPoint effectively for all your future presentations.

What This Book Is About

By working through the sessions in this book, you'll learn about what makes a good presentation and how to use PowerPoint features to organize your ideas. You'll explore tools for formatting text, adding multimedia effects such as sound and animation, and collaborating with others on a presentation project. Finally, you'll learn how to give a great presentation, in person or on the Web. And you'll learn all this in exchange for one weekend of your time.

Who Should Read This Book

Who are you? Let me guess:

- ✿ You're somebody for whom time is at a premium.
- ✿ You're a person who got handed a PowerPoint presentation project Friday afternoon with a deadline of Monday noon to get it done.

OR

- ✿ You don't have a project to do right now, but you want to add knowledge of presentation software to your skill set to be ready when opportunity knocks.
- ✿ You've never used PowerPoint before.

OR

- ✿ You've used a previous version of PowerPoint but not PowerPoint 2002, so you need an update on new features.

If any of these statements fits your profile, this book can help. Whether you are new to creating presentations, are new to PowerPoint, have a current presentation deadline, or just want to learn PowerPoint for future reference, you'll benefit from this book.

One other thing about you: I assume that you have basic computer skills, that you know how to use a mouse and Windows software, and that you can type. (Two fingers is okay....) You don't need to have a master's degree in design or be a great public speaker. You do have to give me your attention for a weekend.

What You Need to Begin

I would like to say that all you need to succeed with this book is your winning personality, but you'll need a couple of other things as well:

- ✿ You need a copy of PowerPoint 2002 installed on your computer or available to you through a company network.

- ✿ It would be useful to have a printer available so you can see what a printed presentation looks like.

- ✿ If you have a presentation of your own to prepare on a tight deadline, keep handy some notes about the contents of that presentation. I've provided a feature called On Your Own that helps you work on your real presentation right alongside our sample presentation so you get practical application of your PowerPoint skills right away.

- ✿ Finally, consider finding a quiet spot in your home where nobody will bother you during your working time.

How This Book Is Organized

I've structured this book in a logical progression, helping you to first organize your presentation contents, then add formatting and graphics, and finally work through settings and multimedia effects you'll need to give your presentation to an audience. Here's what you'll cover in five sessions this weekend:

⚙ **Friday Evening: "Getting Started."** This session explains what makes a good presentation. You'll begin a sample presentation, entering some text in the Normal view of PowerPoint, work with outlining, selecting a design template, and saving the presentation. Finally, you'll learn how to use PowerPoint's Help feature.

⚙ **Saturday Morning: "Creating Your Content."** Here's where you'll start to build your presentation, adding more text and organizing information in both Outline and Slide Sorter views. You'll also learn about PowerPoint's collaboration tools, which allow you to gather and incorporate feedback from others in your presentation and even hold discussions on the Web.

⚙ **Saturday Afternoon: "Working with Design."** This is the afternoon for design! You'll work with design templates and slide layouts to add visual interest and order to information on your PowerPoint slides. This is also where you'll deal with text formatting and learn all about printing your presentation.

⚙ **Sunday Morning: "Adding Visual Interest."** No sleeping late for you: Here's where you start building in elements to back up your ideas, such as charts, tables, and drawings. You'll end this lesson by adding some multimedia spice to catch your audience's attention with animations and sound effects.

⚙ **Sunday Afternoon: "Preparing to Make Your Presentation."** Now that you've built all the pieces of your presentation, you're ready to make settings in this session to give the presentation. You'll set the style of transitions to use between slides, add narration, and learn how to navigate a presentation. This is also the time to learn about making Web-based presentations.

⚙ **Appendix A: "Great Presentations Idea Gallery."** You can explore this appendix to get some ideas for interesting presentations, with examples of great organization and nifty design.

- **Appendix B: "Ten Steps to an Effective Web Presentation."** For those of you who love quick checklists, this appendix provides a handy 10-step summary of what makes a great Web presentation.

- **Appendix C: "Online Resource Directory."** This is a treasure trove of Web addresses where you can get art and media files for your presentation, advice about using PowerPoint, additional PowerPoint design templates, and contact information for slide companies.

- **Appendix D: "Talk the Talk with Speech Recognition."** This appendix describes what you need and how to use it to utilize the speech recognition feature of Office XP.

- **Glossary:** This book uses many terms for PowerPoint features and design elements; I define them when they come up, and this glossary provides an easy way for you to refresh your memory any time you like.

Conventions Used in This Book

To help you make your way through this book in the most streamlined fashion, I've added some special elements that highlight information for efficiency. These include:

CAUTION   **Cautions** generally tell you how to avoid problems.

NOTE   **Notes** provide additional helpful or interesting information.

TIP   **Tips** often suggest techniques and shortcuts to make your life easier.

On Your Own sidebars summarize what you've just done to the sample presentation so you can take a few minutes and update an actual presentation of your own. This means you can work through the sessions and come away from the weekend with a solidly developed presentation you can take back to work and use right away.

Go for It!

One last word of advice before you begin: *Create Microsoft PowerPoint 2002 Presentations In a Weekend* lets you be a graphic designer, a writer, a multimedia developer, and a Web author, so have fun with it. A positive approach can make the weekend fly!

Get Ready, Get Set...

- ✪ Learning what makes a good presentation
- ✪ Creating your first presentation
- ✪ Entering text on a slide
- ✪ Applying a design template
- ✪ Saving a presentation
- ✪ Learning what PowerPoint's Help system has to offer

Second only to those dreaded words, "Hey, I want you to make a presentation..." are the words, "Hey, I want you to prepare a presentation." If somebody has let you know you're elected to do just that and your presentation skills are shaky, never fear. In just one weekend, I will take you by the hand and help you create a presentation that will blow away your audience.

Presentations are, at their simplest, collections of ideas that help persuade, inform, or motivate people. In the past, presentations have been essentially a series of bullet-point lists that help an audience follow a live presenter's train of thought. But today's presentation technology allows you to move far beyond the simple overhead display and wooden pointer routine. Today, you can post standalone presentations on the Web; loop presentations to show repeatedly at trade-show booths; burn CDs of your presentation to distribute to your audience; add animation, sound, and even video to your slides; and do it all easily from 20 cities in 17 days, on the Web in real time, or in the comfort of your own conference room.

Over this weekend, I take you one step at a time through all the tools PowerPoint puts at your disposal to create an effective presentation, building the layers of words and multimedia that help you to get your message across. Your first step this Friday evening is to find a comfy, private place to work, disconnect the phone, and ask your family to keep the volume down on the TV. Your second step is to prepare for your presentation before you even open PowerPoint.

What Makes a Good Presentation?

Presentation software such as PowerPoint has made creating presentations easier than ever. But this ubiquitous access to presentation tools also presents you with a challenge: Every Tom, Dick, and Mary is using PowerPoint or some other software to create presentations. The same backgrounds, clip art, and phrases turn up at every sales conference and corporate seminar. How do you make sure your presentation is better than everybody else's?

I'd like to say you can make your presentation stand out by using stunning animated graphics and sound clips of rap music. Those are entertaining, but they're not the foundation of a great presentation. The place you have to start is a little less glitzy. You have to begin with old-fashioned planning and good, solid content, because when all is said and done, it's the ideas you put forth that should stick in the audience's minds, not the 3-D rotating picture of Britney Spears.

NOTE The variety of people who may be involved in creating a presentation is a dynamic you should be aware of right from the outset. There are some people who still write, design, and present their own presentations. But today there is often one person (or a team of people) contributing content, another person or persons fine-tuning design elements, and seven different people presenting the slide show in seven different locales. In this book you'll wear all the hats, but be alert to PowerPoint collaboration tools as a way to orchestrate a presentation project if you're only a cog in a PowerPoint wheel.

And Our Topic Tonight Is...

You might think you know the topic of your presentation, but think again. Think not just about what your boss told you to do (a sales presentation, a report on your project's progress, or a new product launch), but about what you want your presentation to accomplish. For example, the following list shows you the many focuses a new product launch presentation might have:

- ✪ To outline the timeline and deliverables of the product launch to the manufacturing team.
- ✪ To teach the sales force about the features and benefits of the new product so they're prepared to sell it. (Figure 1.1 shows a slide that uses this kind of informational approach.)
- ✪ To make a business case about the potential market for the new product to gain financing from investors. (The slide in Figure 1.2 contains this kind of motivational content.)
- ✪ To introduce the new product to customers.

Once you figure out your topic and the focus you will give it, you also have to pin down the scope of the presentation. Scope simply means how long and detailed the information you present will be. Scope is defined by the designated time you have to present the information, the attention span of the audience, and the purpose of the presentation. If your presentation will provide an overview of a new procedure, you might decide to leave the step-by-step details to the employee manual. If you are supposed to give a breakdown of quarterly financials to senior management, you might want to include detailed charts or lists of numbers (but always back these up with printed handouts for reference). The point is you must consider the amount and level of information that is right for your topic before you begin.

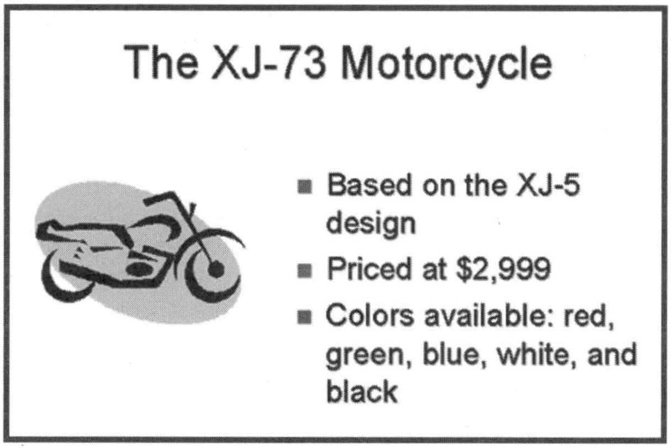

Figure 1.1

The approach of this slide is informational...

The XJ-73 Motorcycle

- ■ Based on the XJ-5 design
- ■ Priced at $2,999
- ■ Colors available: red, green, blue, white, and black

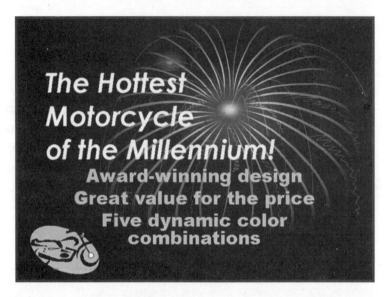

Figure 1.2

...whereas this slide is motivational.

Remember that most people retain only a small percentage of information you give in any presentation. In most cases, you'll hit the high points and reinforce them with printed material they can refer to at a later time.

Knowing Your Audience

Knowing your audience is a truism that's right up there with "Don't run with scissors"—and every bit as important. If you don't know to whom you will present, you can't be a very effective presenter. That's because a presentation is a two-way street; if the audience is bored or upset by what you say, no matter how well you say it, your presentation will be a flop.

Here are some reasons for doing your audience homework. You should have a good idea about who will be in your audience so:

- You can use or avoid technical or specialized jargon with which the audience might or might not be familiar.

- You know what assumptions you can make about what your audience already knows and what they need you to explain to them.

✪ You have a clue about how this audience will react to your presentation; if they will be resistant or resentful to your ideas, you might need to win their buy-in by organizing or presenting information differently (see Figure 1.3).

✪ You know their motivations for attending your presentation; were they forced to attend by their boss, do they need to be there to keep their job or get a promotion, or are they truly excited about what you have to say? If your audience feels that you understand their situation, they are more sympathetic to you as a presenter.

Getting Your Content Ducks in a Row

There's nothing deadlier than sitting through a presentation when the presenter doesn't know a thing about his or her topic and the content of the slides consists of vague platitudes. You have to do your homework to make your bullet points worth reading and your supporting comments (if you're doing a live presentation) useful. Most live presentations allow for a question-and-answer session at some point, so be prepared to answer detailed questions about topics only summarized in your presentation material.

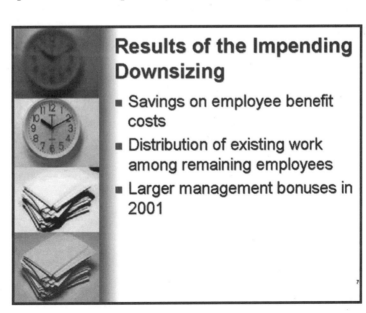

Figure 1.3

How would this slide be received by the worker's union? How about by senior management?

Results of the Impending Downsizing

- Savings on employee benefit costs
- Distribution of existing work among remaining employees
- Larger management bonuses in 2001

Here are a few tips for good content:

- Be specific. If you quote a specific statistic, provide the source to give it credibility.
- Avoid clichés.
- Be concise and clear in your titles and bullet points.
- If you make an assertion, have the facts you need to show how you reached that conclusion.
- If you give examples, and especially if you mention people by name in your examples, be sure you have the facts straight.
- If you don't know the answer to something, don't fake it; tell your audience you will check on it and e-mail them later with the answer.

Organizing Your Information

People's minds work in patterns, searching subconsciously for some coherence, order, and flow to information. If you don't provide the order, your audience's minds impose an order of their own. That can be especially disastrous in a persuasive presentation where you can leave an audience drawing the wrong conclusion because you didn't place the emphasis where you wanted it to be.

You can make your audience feel more comfortable and help them follow your ideas if you build in an order up front. Information naturally falls into certain patterns, which you might apply over an entire presentation or slide-by-slide:

- Chronological—You use the order that things occurred in time, as in the slide content in Figure 1.4.
- Spatial—You use the order in which things appear in space in relation to each other, such as the order in which rooms flow when discussing the floor plan for a new office.
- Priority—You work from the most important point to the least important.

How We Got Where We Are Today

- New product line launched in 1987
- Owned majority market share by 1992
- Competition came out with less expensive product in 1995
- Sales decreased significantly by 1997
- Lost more market share in 2000 after recalls

Figure 1.4

To organize information, you can put it in the context of time.

✿ Cause and effect—You show how a result naturally proceeded from some action or situation.

If you can find a hook into one of these patterns—say, giving a project-update presentation by starting with how the project began and leading up to the present in chronological order—use it.

Another trick is to organize details and conclusions. As a rule, if you want to persuade somebody, offer the facts and then give the conclusion. In that way, you walk the listener through your argument so that he or she reaches the conclusion with you. If you're giving a more informative presentation, it might be better to present the conclusions that are really the most important information for the audience to retain and then provide the details to support them.

TIP

PowerPoint's Outline feature is a great tool for helping you to organize your presentation to create a logical flow to your content, and the Slide Sorter View helps you rearrange major ideas after you've built your first draft outline. You'll learn more about each in tomorrow's sessions.

Understanding PowerPoint's Output Options

To build the best presentation, you have to anticipate where and how your presentation will be given. Some important things to consider are:

○ Will you have equipment that makes sound and video playback possible? If you can't play a sound file, don't waste time building sound clips into your presentation.

○ Will sound or video play at a fast enough speed to be effective? The amount of memory and processor speed on your computer affects this. To play back a video, you should have at least a Pentium-level processor, for example.

○ Will you be able to connect to the Internet during the presentation so that embedding links to Web sites in your slides makes sense?

○ Will you be at the presentation, or will your presentation play by itself on the Web or a computer display? A standalone presentation requires more complete ideas and information than one backed up by a live presenter's comments.

○ Will somebody else make the presentation? If so, you probably need to place notes within the presentation that give the speaker the background data he or she might need to reinforce the slide content.

○ Will the presentation happen in a very large room, making reading your slides problematic, or in a more intimate setting? The further the audience is from your slides, the larger your presentation display and even text size must be.

○ Will your presentation use a slide projector, a computer attached to a projection system, a computer screen displayed at a trade show kiosk, or a computer connected to a large format television?

○ Will the room for your presentation be dark or bright? That can affect the colors you choose for text and background. For example, in a bright room pastel shades may fade out; in this case a simple palette with dark or bright colors would be preferable.

ON YOUR OWN: GETTING READY

If you're creating your own presentation as you follow along with this book, you should fill out the following worksheet to plan the structure of your content and keep it handy over the next few days:

1. What is my topic? (For example, is it a sales presentation to inform or a customer presentation to persuade?)

2. What is the scope of my presentation?

    * How much time do I have to present?

    * What level of detail is necessary?

    * What does my audience need to be able to do after the presentation? (For example, should they come away with a general understanding, know how to implement a process, or comprehend a strategy?)

3. Who is my audience?

    * What terminology or jargon do they know?

    * What do they already know about the topic?

    * What will they do with the information?

    * Why are they attending the presentation?

    * How do they feel about my topic?

4. Where will I research my content? (Will I use company records, the Internet, project notes, an expert interview, and so on?)

5. How will I organize my content? (Will I organize it chronologically, by cause and effect, and so on?)

6. Describe the environment where the presentation will take place and the equipment that will be available:

Taking a Break

Okay, you've earned a break. You've learned about laying the groundwork for a well-thought-out presentation. Go get a soda, check your voicemail, and get back here so you can begin to fire up PowerPoint and get to work!

A First Glimpse of PowerPoint 2002

It's time to introduce you to PowerPoint's environment, giving you an overview of the tools and features you'll be using as you build your presentation. There are three major ways of getting things done in Power-Point:

✪ Toolbars provide one-click access to most of the common functions in PowerPoint.

✪ Menus provide a text-based way to access features, and in some cases make some more advanced settings than are available with toolbars.

✪ Panes, which are new to PowerPoint 2002, provide context-specific sets of tools and menus to help you complete the type of task you're currently working on, such as setting the slide design or opening a presentation.

Taking a Look at PowerPoint's Toolbars

When you first open PowerPoint by selecting the Windows Start menu, Programs, and then choosing Microsoft PowerPoint from the Programs submenu, you see a blank presentation, as shown in Figure 1.5.

You can display any toolbar by selecting View, Toolbars and choosing the toolbar you want to display by selecting it from the side menu that appears. When a toolbar is selected for display, a boxed checkmark appears next to it. To hide a toolbar, just return to the View menu, select Toolbars, and clear any checked toolbar item to hide it.

Standard toolbar

Formatting toolbar

Drawing toolbar

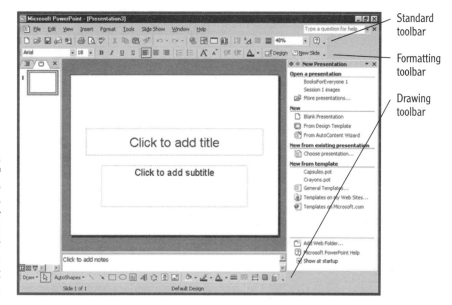

Figure 1.5

Some of the tools PowerPoint makes available for working on a presentation may be familiar from other Microsoft programs.

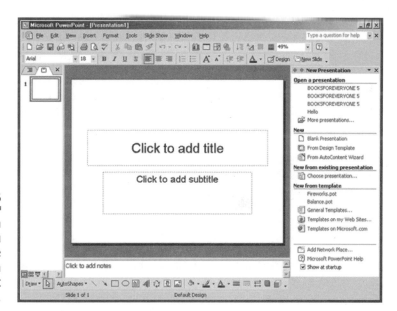

Figure 1.6

The name of each tool appears as you scroll your mouse cursor over it on your PowerPoint screen.

The three toolbars you'll work with most are the Standard toolbar, Formatting toolbar, and Drawing toolbar, which you can see in detail in Figure 1.6:

- The Standard toolbar contains tools for working with files, text, and objects, such as Save, Print, Cut, Copy, Undo, Insert Table, and Zoom.

- The Formatting toolbar is just that: It offers you tools for formatting text and objects in your presentation, modifying font, alignment, color, and so on.

- The Drawing toolbar contains drawing tools. These tools allow you to draw objects on a slide, format those objects, and control their rotation and arrangement on the slide.

MODIFYING TOOLBAR SETTINGS

Toolbars aren't static things. You can hide or display various toolbars by selecting View, Toolbars and selecting the toolbar you want from the side menu that appears. You can also add or remove tools that are contained on each toolbar by right-clicking on a toolbar, selecting Customize, and then using the Commands tab of the Toolbar dialog box to add or delete commands to a selected toolbar. I advise you not to make too many changes to default settings until you get more comfortable with PowerPoint, however.

You'll also notice that sometimes a tool you'd like to use isn't visible; that's because Microsoft has actually included more tools in many cases than a single toolbar can display on-screen at one time. Note the small arrow on the right-hand side of each of these toolbars. By clicking on that arrow, you display a few more tools that don't fit on-screen by default, but that you might want to use from time to time. Once you use a hidden tool, Microsoft keeps it on the visible portion of the toolbar; any tool you use on a regular basis will be kept visible at all times.

What's on the Menu?

There is a great deal of crossover between tools and menus: You can accomplish just about every function in PowerPoint by using either a menu command or performing the same function by clicking on a tool. In several cases, however, opting for the menu route provides the ability to work with more detailed settings through dialog boxes.

The nine menus displayed across the top of the PowerPoint screen allow you to select actions by commands. In some cases, selecting a command on a menu displays a side menu of additional choices, as with the Online Collaboration selection shown in Figure 1.7. Note that PowerPoint does not automatically display the entire menu. It displays the most frequently used commands and provides two down arrows at the bottom of the menu; you can click on these arrows to reveal the entire menu.

TIP You can also change how menus display by selecting View, Toolbars, Customize. Click on the Options tab to display it, and select either Always show full menus, or Show full menus after a short delay.

Notice several menu commands have notations such as F5 or Ctrl+M. You can use these keystroke shortcuts to perform the same function. F5 refers to a function key along the top of your keyboard; Ctrl+M means that you press your Ctrl key and, while holding it down, also press the letter M.

Figure 1.7

Displaying only the most commonly used commands can make it easier to spot a frequently used item more quickly.

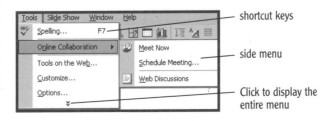

shortcut keys

side menu

Click to display the entire menu

TIP You can set keystroke shortcuts to display along with ToolTips (the little balloon message that tells you the name of a tool when you hover your mouse over it) by selecting View, Toolbars, Customize. Click on the Options tab to display it, and select Show Shortcut Keys in ScreenTips.

Finally, note the corresponding tool icon displayed to the left of many commands. This helps you begin to memorize tool functions as you work with PowerPoint menus.

Table 1.1 provides an overview of the typical functions included in each menu.

Getting Things Done with Task Panes

You perform most activities in PowerPoint using tools or menus. However, in PowerPoint 2002, Microsoft has also provided a new feature called task panes; these panes gather together tools and menu choices related to a specific type of activity. New Presentation, Revisions, Slide Design, and Slide Layout are just some of the task panes available to you. Task panes appear along the right side of the PowerPoint screen. The Slide Design task pane appears in Figure 1.8.

In most cases, you can just sit back and let PowerPoint display task panes relevant to tasks you're performing. For example, when you open Power-Point, the New Presentation task pane will appear automatically, offering you the option of opening a recently used presentation, a blank presentation, or a presentation based on a template. In other cases, initiating a menu command causes a task pane to appear; for example, if you select Format, Slide Design, the Slide Design task pane appears.

TABLE 1.1 POWERPOINT MENU COMMANDS

Menu	Types of Commands
File	Open new and existing files; save and close files; save a file as a Web page; preview a Web presentation; make page and printing settings; and so on.
Edit	Undo and repeat actions; cut, copy, and paste text and objects; open the Office Clipboard; paste a hyperlink; duplicate and delete slides; find and replace text; and work with links and objects.
View	Display various PowerPoint views; adjust on-screen color; display or hide rulers, toolbars, and grids; access the header/footer feature; and zoom in or out.
Insert	Place a variety of items on your page, such as the date and time, symbols, comments, pictures, diagrams, charts, hyperlinks, or tables; insert a new or duplicate slide; insert slides from other files.
Format	Work with fonts, bulleted and numbered lists, and alignment on your slides; display the Slide Design and Slide Layout task panes; display the background dialog box; and format objects.
Tools	Access Web tools; compare and merge presentations; use spelling and language tools; record macros; adjust AutoCorrect and other PowerPoint functions and options.
Slide Show	Generally work with settings for running slide shows, such as timings, narration, online broadcast, transitions, and animations.
Window	Arrange windows on your screen or quickly open previously opened files.
Help	Access online and offline help tools.

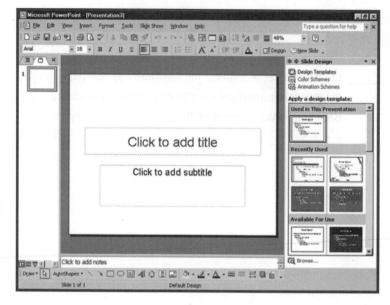

Figure 1.8

Task panes such as
this one offer a
series of choices in
a handy on-screen
list format.

Here are some of the task panes that appear as a result of selecting a menu command:

- File, New (New Presentation task pane)
- View, Toolbars, Revisions Pane (Revisions task pane)
- Format, Slide Design (Slide Design task pane)
- Format, Slide Layout (Slide Layout task pane)

No matter how a pane appears, you use the menus and tools in the task panes just as you would other menus and tools, but you have the convenience of working with them all in one place. In some cases, task panes also contain previews of designs, graphic images, or layouts that make selections easier to browse and insert. Although task panes may take a little getting used to, they can make your PowerPoint experience easier in the end.

TIP You can resize any displayed task pane by moving your mouse over the left edge of it until the cursor turns into a double pointing arrow, then clicking and dragging to make the pane larger or smaller. You can close any task pane by clicking the Close button in the top-right corner; you can move to previously displayed task panes by clicking on the Back and Forward arrows on the top-left side of any pane.

TIP You can also quickly display the Slide Design task pane by clicking on the Slide Design tool on the Formatting toolbar.

Creating a New Presentation

The sample presentation you'll build this weekend is for an Internet start-up Web site called BooksForEveryone.com. BooksForEveryone.com is a Web site for people who love to read. It will include discounted electronic books, links to bookstores and publishers, and an online store with products of interest to readers such as book lights, highlighters, and bookstands. The site will also include weekly columns by writers, as well as book reviews.

You're preparing a presentation that you will give to potential investors. These sophisticated business people are on the cutting edge of Internet technology. The presentation scope includes outlining the offerings on Books-ForEveryone.com, profiling the potential market for the site, and explaining the profit model. You have half an hour to make the presentation.

The goal of the presentation is to get investors excited about the potential market for the site and interest them in investing in the company. You will give the presentation in hotel conference rooms at various locations around the country, with an audience of no more than 20 people at a time. You will use a computer projection system with the capability of handling complex multimedia effects and linking to the Web.

Now that you've got the background on the presentation, you can get started. Remember, if you also want to build your own presentation as we go this weekend, complete the On Your Own steps whenever they appear.

Using the New Presentation Task Pane

When you first open PowerPoint, you see a blank title slide and the New Presentation task pane along the right side of the page. This pane, shown in Figure 1.9, offers options for working on presentations, including:

○ Opening an existing presentation

○ Opening a blank presentation, applying a design template to the current blank presentation, or using the AutoContent Wizard to create a presentation with suggested content already in place

○ Opening a new presentation based on an existing presentation

○ Opening a new presentation from a template

Figure 1.9

The New Presentation task pane offers several choices for selecting and working on a presentation.

Note that although you have the option of opening a new, blank presentation, when you first open PowerPoint, a new, blank presentation opens automatically.

NOTE If you've used earlier versions of PowerPoint, you'll notice that the New Presentation task pane is new to PowerPoint 2002. In past versions of PowerPoint, you saw a dialog box before you saw the main PowerPoint screen; this dialog box offered you the option of choosing the layout of the first slide in a new, blank presentation or of opening an existing presentation. In PowerPoint 2002, the dialog box is gone. Instead, you are immediately given a blank presentation, and the first slide appears with the Title Slide layout already applied.

Exploring Your Options for Creating a Presentation

Consider for a moment the several ways PowerPoint offers to begin to build a slide show.

Selecting a Blank Presentation gives you a single title slide with no design applied and no content entered.

Selecting the Design Template option in the New Presentations task pane opens the Slide Design task pane, which offers you a choice of several designs you can apply to your already open, blank presentation. These designs can include graphic elements, a slide background color or pattern, and font settings.

The AutoContent Wizard asks you a few questions about your presentation in a series of dialog boxes, such as the one shown in Figure 1.10, and then creates a presentation based on your input using a content template.

The presentation generated by AutoContent Wizard includes a title slide whose text you enter within one of the wizard's dialog boxes and slides with placeholders for text based on the type of presentation you selected.

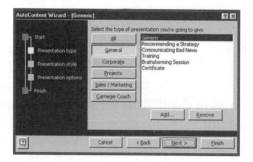

Figure 1.10

PowerPoint's AutoContent Wizard walks you through the creation of a new presentation.

In the slide and outline shown in Figure 1.11, for example, the presentation type I selected was Projects. PowerPoint then provided content suggestions in a series of eleven slides.

Selecting a Design Background

Because you're now looking at a new, blank presentation that appeared when you opened PowerPoint, you'll start working on that presentation by selecting a design for the slides. PowerPoint contains several slide designs, and you can easily try a few on for size to see which matches your

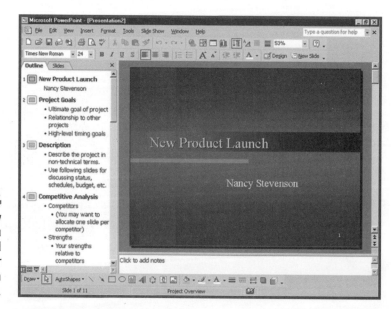

Figure 1.11

The slides already created for you give you a head start on your presentation content.

presentation's topic and audience. Click on the From Design Template item in the New Presentation task pane. The Slide Design task pane appears, as shown in Figure 1.12.

When you place your mouse cursor over a design, its name appears. Notice that the styles of the designs vary from very dark in background (such as the design titled Stream) to very light (Network) and from more conservative and businesslike (Blends) to creative and fun (Crayons). Use the scrollbar in the Slide Design task pane to display additional designs.

TIP If you want to locate even more design templates by downloading them from the Office XP CD or from the Web, scroll down to the bottom of the Apply a Design Template area and click on Additional Design Templates.

Figure 1.12

The Slide Design task pane replaces the New Presentation task pane on the right side of your screen.

You can apply a design by following these steps:

1. Click on the arrow on the right side of any slide design preview; a drop-down menu appears.

2. Select the Apply to All Slides option. The selected design appears on all slides in your presentation.

Note that if you ever want to use this method to apply a design to a single slide in a presentation rather than all the slides, you would select Apply to Selected Slides from the preview drop-down menu.

TIP   Here's a shortcut: You can also click on any design preview to instantly apply it to all slides. But use the preview drop-down menu if you want to apply your design to selected slides.

Take a moment to click on various previews to apply different designs to your presentation and get a feel for what's available. After you've played around with applying a few different designs, it's time to get down to business and apply a design for the BooksForEveryone.com presentation. Because this presentation has a high-tech topic and audience and will be shown in conference rooms that aren't very dark, the best design choice is a lighter background with a contemporary look, such as Capsules. Apply Capsules now by locating it in the Slide Design task pane and clicking on it. Your slide should look like the one shown in Figure 1.13.

Entering Text on Your Title Slide

Okay, are you ready for something easy to do? Entering text on a slide is just about as easy as it gets. When you opened PowerPoint, it automatically created a blank presentation with a single slide. That slide uses the Title Slide layout, with a text placeholder for a title and another for a subtitle. Slide layouts can contain text placeholders for titles, subtitles and

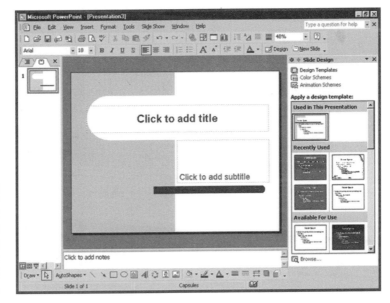

Figure 1.13

The clean, graphic lines of the Capsules design gives a high-tech feeling to the presentation.

bullet points, content placeholders that allow you to insert graphics, charts, and multimedia, or a combination of the two. (You'll learn more about slide layouts tomorrow morning.)

To enter the title for your presentation, follow these steps:

1. Click on the object labeled Click to add title. The placeholder text disappears, and the text box is open, ready for you to enter text.

2. Type this: BooksForEveryone.com.

3. Click on the object labeled Click to add subtitle. The placeholder text again disappears and the text box opens.

4. Type today's date.

5. Click anywhere outside of the two text boxes, and your slide should look like the one shown in Figure 1.14.

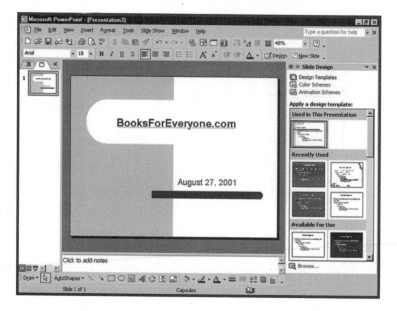

Figure 1.14

By entering slide text, you're on your way to creating your first presentation.

Notice that the term BooksForEveryone.com has a faint red underline. That indicates that PowerPoint has flagged this word as possibly being a misspelling. Because this is a proper name (and a run-together Web site name at that) and although it is correct it, doesn't make sense to PowerPoint's spelling function. You can stop PowerPoint from checking spelling as you work on your presentation by selecting Tools, Options, and on the Spelling & Style tab, check the Check Spelling As You Type option to deselect it.

Saving the Presentation

Now that you've made some presentation choices, it's smart to save the presentation so you can work on it again tomorrow. Here's all you have to do:

1. Select File, Save, or simply click on the Save icon.

2. In the Save As dialog box shown in Figure 1.15, enter the file name BooksForEveryone 1, to designate the file you save for Session 1 of this book.

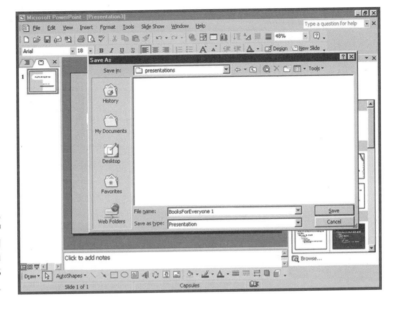

Figure 1.15

The Save As dialog box is a common sight in Windows applications.

3. Locate the place on your hard drive where you'd like to save the file by using the Save in drop-down list.

4. When you have found the location where you'd like to save the file, click on the Create New Folder tool at the top of the Save As dialog box.

5. Enter the name of the new folder, Presentations, and click OK.

6. Click Save to save the file with the name you entered in the new folder. (Whenever you save a version of our sample presentation this weekend, save it to this folder so you can find it easily.)

ON YOUR OWN: CREATE YOUR OWN PRESENTATION

If you're building your own presentation as you go, follow these steps to create your own new presentation:

1. Open PowerPoint by opening the Start menu from the Windows desktop and then selecting Programs, Microsoft PowerPoint 2002. A new, blank presentation opens.

2. Click on the From Design Template in the New Presentations task pane, and click on a design to apply it to your entire presentation.

3. Click on the Title placeholder on the blank title slide that was created automatically when you opened PowerPoint, and type your presentation title.

4. Repeat the process used in Step 3 with the Subtitle placeholder to enter a presentation subtitle.

5. Save your presentation in a location and with a name of your choice.

That's it!

Help!

Before I send you off to bed, or to watch one last rerun of The X-Files, I want to acquaint you with some of PowerPoint's help features. These features might come in handy as you jump into some serious presentation design in the next couple of days, and knowing about them will undoubtedly help you sleep better tonight!

TIP If you know Microsoft help features as well as you know your 80-year-old Aunt Tilly, you can probably skip this section and get on with your life. Except for a little reorganization of information, the Help system should be familiar. The Answer Wizard is the only new Help feature in this version of PowerPoint you might take a look at.

Making Friends with the Office Assistant

It's like opera: Some people love it and some people hate it, but few people are lukewarm on the topic. However you feel about it, the little paper-clip character called Office Assistant that Microsoft has placed inside your computer offers one way to access help when you need it.

The Office Assistant is a feature that can magically appear whenever you seem to be at a loss for what to do next. Basically, if you try repeatedly to do an action, or do it in the least efficient way, a little animated character (see Figure 1.16) pops up on your screen, asks what you're trying to do, and offers suggested help topics. The good news is that Office Assistant is sometimes helpful. The other good news is that you can turn it off if it starts to annoy you. You can do so by right-clicking on it and selecting Hide from the shortcut menu that appears.

Here's the low-down on using Office Assistant:

○ The Office Assistant appears by itself if it thinks you need help, but if you want to turn it on yourself to customize how it acts, select Help, Show the Office Assistant, and then right-click on it and select Options from the shortcut menu that appears.

○ You can display the Office Assistant by selecting Help, Microsoft PowerPoint Help. It appears in the upper-right corner of the screen. If you access it this way, the Assistant simply offers a small pop-up box where you can enter a question; there's also a Search button here that takes you to a Help search screen.

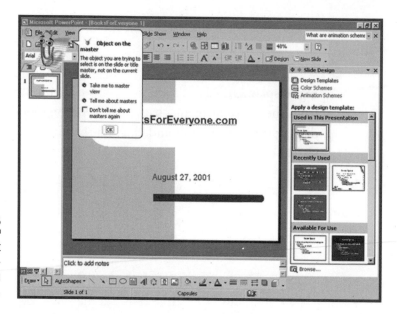

Figure 1.16

Office Assistant tries to second-guess what you need help with.

- When the Office Assistant is displayed automatically, it might offer a list of help topics associated with what you're trying to accomplish (but it might not). If it does, just click on a topic that's relevant to display help information.

- If Office Assistant doesn't provide a list of suggested topics (or if it does but none is what you need), type a question in the Answer Wizard box at the top-right corner of the screen (see Figure 1.17), which says "Type a question for help." Press Enter and a drop-down list of possible topics appears. Click on any topic to read detailed help suggestions.

Figure 1.17

Ask a question in plain old English, and PowerPoint offers suggested help topics.

- To hide the Office Assistant once it's displayed, right-click on it, and select Hide from the shortcut menu that appears.

- If you've had enough and you want to send the little fellow packing, display Office Assistant and right-click on it. Select Options from the shortcut menu that appears. In the Options dialog box, display the Options tab and click on the Use the Office Assistant checkbox to clear it.

 TIP You can change other settings in the Options dialog box, including the criteria for when Office Assistant pops up and what your Office Assistant looks like by selecting another character from the Office Assistant Gallery.

Using Microsoft PowerPoint Help

When you select Help, Microsoft PowerPoint Help, if you have not deactivated the Office Assistant, the Assistant appears; you can then click on a help topic or type a question and click Search to go to Microsoft PowerPoint Help. If you have turned off the Office Assistant feature, when you select Help, Microsoft PowerPoint Help, you go directly to the Microsoft PowerPoint Help screen shown in Figure 1.18. To enlarge the display to fill your screen, click the Maximize button in the top-right corner of the window.

The PowerPoint Help system consists of four main areas:

- Contents—A searchable table of contents consisting of help topics.

- Answer Wizard—A natural-language interface feature that allows you to type in a question and click on the Search button to get a list of suggested help topics.

- Index—A searchable book-like index, where you search by keyword, rather than by topic.

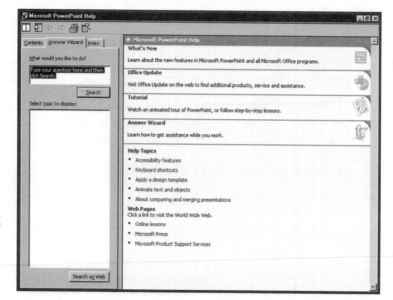

Figure 1.18

The familiar help
system is common
to many Microsoft
products.

✪   The pane on the right of the Help screen—Kind of a Help central;
it lists links to information, including what's new in this version of
PowerPoint, the online Office Update page, an animated tutorial,
and the Answer Wizard. This area also offers suggested help topics
and Web page links you can click to visit online help sources.
When you select a specific topic through the Contents or Index,
the help information is displayed in this space.

NOTE   When you follow a series of more and more detailed topics through the Contents section, click on a suggested help topic in the Answer Wizard or Office Assistant, or select a
specific topic from the Index, you eventually end up at the same place: a detailed help
topic explanation. Microsoft simply provides all these different help features to allow
users to get to this information in different ways, much as a book offers both a table of
contents and index to get to information on a particular page.

Whichever method you choose to get to help information, after you've read about a topic, you can close the PowerPoint Help window by clicking the Close button in the top-right corner. If you prefer, you can minimize the Help window and leave it on-screen as you work by clicking the Restore button.

Getting Help Online

If you want to head right to the Web to do your help surfing, PowerPoint lets you do that. Select Help, Office on the Web. This takes you to the Office Update Worldwide site. From there, you can click on the Support tab to see the support options shown in Figure 1.19.

On this Web page, which will change its contents periodically, you can search Microsoft's Knowledge Base, a larger help database than is included with PowerPoint. You can also look for free downloads of product updates, find phone numbers so you can call a real person for help, e-mail an online support request, or review a frequently-asked-questions section.

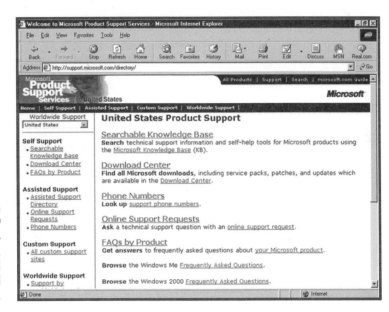

Figure 1.19

Microsoft offers help, information, updates, and additional templates online.

TIP You can also go to Web help by clicking the Search on Web button displayed in the Microsoft PowerPoint Help window.

Closing PowerPoint

Now that you've saved your work, you can close PowerPoint by clicking the Close button in the top-right corner. You can also select the File menu and choose the Exit command.

NOTE If you had not already saved your presentation, PowerPoint would have prompted you after either of the preceding steps and asked whether you want to save the presentation. It's just a little safety net to help make sure you don't lose your work!

What's Next?

Well done! You've finished your first session a little wiser about how a PowerPoint presentation comes together and with a new presentation saved, ready to fill in the details. Here's what you have to look forward to tomorrow morning:

- ✿ Adding new slides to your presentation and working with slide layouts.
- ✿ Working with the Outline feature in the Normal view to add and organize presentation content.
- ✿ Taking a look at new collaboration tools that help several people provide input on a single presentation.

Sleep tight!

Creating Your Content

- ✿ Building a presentation outline
- ✿ Reorganizing content in Normal and Slide Sorter views
- ✿ Adding, deleting, and duplicating slides
- ✿ Working with collaboration tools

I'm glad to see that you've kept your resolve to learn PowerPoint and delayed that Saturday morning trip to the mall or mountain bike ride until another time. Good for you. This morning, you're going to get hands on with your PowerPoint presentation.

Remember that the sample presentation you begin to build today will be used to inform and persuade investors to fund a new Web site, BooksForEveryone.com. Time to get started.

Word Play

Although multimedia objects and effects are fun to watch, the majority of your message hangs on the infrastructure of words. So start the sample presentation by trying different methods of entering text into Power-Point. You can enter text directly onto individual slides or in Normal view on the Outline tab. In the early stages of drafting your presentation, when you need to enter a great deal of text at once, the outline is probably your best choice. It lets you enter all text in one location and helps you to focus on the structure of your ideas, rather than the design of your slides.

Opening Your Presentation

Start by opening PowerPoint (Start, Programs, Microsoft PowerPoint 2002). Select the file you saved last night (BooksForEveryone 1) from the list of recently opened files in the Open a Presentation list. (If you didn't save this file, you can open the file with the same name on the CD that accompanies this book. Use the File, Open command and locate the file on your CD drive.)

TIP   You can also see a list of recently opened presentations on the File menu. The list of recently used files near the bottom of this menu can include up to nine items. You can increase the number of files shown by adjusting the Recently Used File List counter on the General tab of the PowerPoint Options dialog box (Tools, Options).

Exploring the Outline Feature of PowerPoint

An outline is a simple organizational device that helps you put the ideas for your presentation into a hierarchical order, placing main topics furthest to the left and the details of those topics at a lower level of the hierarchy further to the right. The presentation outline is contained within a pane in Normal view. Click on the Normal view icon in the lower-left corner of the PowerPoint screen, and you'll see one large pane with the selected slide displayed, and to its left a pane that contains an Outline tab and Slide tab. Click on the Outline tab and the presentation outline appears. You currently see one heading and one subheading, corresponding to the text you entered on the title slide last night. To display the Outlining toolbar, select View, Toolbars, Outlining. Your screen will now look like the one shown in Figure 2.1.

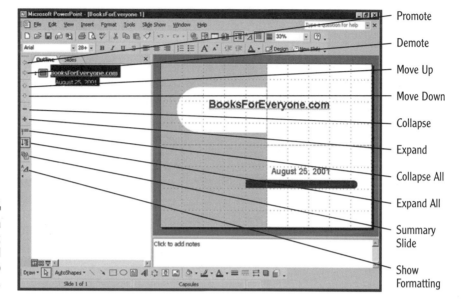

Promote

Demote

Move Up

Move Down

Collapse

Expand

Collapse All

Expand All

Summary Slide

Show Formatting

Figure 2.1

Each main idea receives a number; each lower-level item is indented to the right.

Entering Text

Start entering text for your presentation within the Outline by following these steps:

1. Click to the right of the last line of text in the outline, if your cursor isn't already resting there.

2. Press Enter to create a new line in the outline. Notice that when you press Enter, the heading you create appears at the same level of the outline as the heading before it.

3. Type the heading **BooksForEveryone.com: The Place for the Serious Reader**. Your outline should look like the one shown in Figure 2.2.

4. Now save the file with the name BooksForEveryone 2.

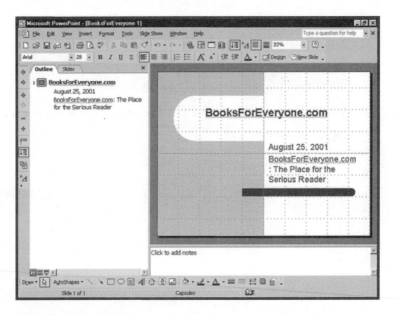

Figure 2.2

Focusing on the Outline while entering text helps you put aside concerns about design, such as how text breaks from line to line on your slide.

Selecting Text and Slides

You've been selecting text since you used your first Windows program, so you know all about clicking in front or at the end of text you want to select, holding down your mouse button and dragging across the text to select it. Selected text is highlighted, and whatever you do next, such as applying formatting or pressing the Delete key, happens to the selected text. Things work that way in PowerPoint, too. However, selecting a slide—not the text on the slide, but the slide itself—works a bit differently.

A slide is an object. Even in the outline for a presentation, each slide can be selected as an entire object for the purpose of moving, duplicating, or deleting it. In the outline there is a small slide icon to the left of each slide. To select the slide (rather than the text on the slide) you simply click on that icon.

The other place where you can select a slide to move, duplicate, or delete is where you use Slide Sorter view, which you explore later in this book. In that view, you simply click on any slide to select it. Note that in Slide Sorter view you cannot select text on a slide at all; that must be done in Normal view.

TIP

You can also hold down the Shift key as you click on any number of contiguous slides to select all of them, or hold down the Ctrl key as you click on non-contiguous slides to select several at once.

Promoting and Demoting Headings

Just as a general creates order in the ranks, to create the hierarchy of an outline you have to be able to move headings to different levels. This creates a visual structure for information. To change heading levels, you use two tools in PowerPoint called Promote and Demote. The Promote tool moves a heading to the left, designating it as a higher-level topic. The Demote tool moves a heading to the right, placing it at a lower level in the hierarchy.

NOTE

Although you can theoretically have dozens of levels of detail in a PowerPoint outline, avoid it. The limited space of a PowerPoint slide doesn't lend itself to too many levels of information. Instead, if you find several levels of information under a single topic heading, consider breaking up the topic into several subtopics on separate slides.

Use one of these tools now. With your cursor resting anywhere on the line of the heading you just entered, click the Promote tool in the Outline toolbar. This moves that heading up in the outline hierarchy.

TIP

You can also use the shortcut keys Shift+Tab to promote a heading and Tab to demote a heading.

Promoting makes this heading a main topic in the outline and creates a new slide. Once you've created a title slide for a presentation, every new slide you create uses the Text layout by default, which includes a title and bulleted list.

Entering Text

Now it's time for some plain, unglamorous practice in entering text using PowerPoint's Outline. Enter the text shown in the outline section of Figure 2.3, promoting and demoting headings as indicated.

Remember these procedures as you build your outline:

✿ When you press Enter, PowerPoint creates a new heading at the same level as the heading before it. If you want a heading to start a new slide, use the Promote tool to move it up to the top level in the outline.

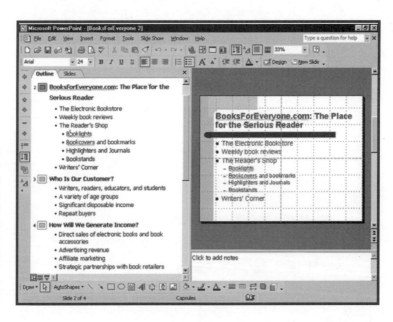

Figure 2.3

These slides represent the three main areas of discussion for this presentation: the contents of the Web site, the market for the site, and the profit model.

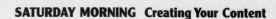

- ✿ To demote a heading, you can select it and then use the Demote button or press Tab.

- ✿ You can create additional levels of detail by demoting a heading more than once.

- ✿ If you create a bullet point for a topic, you must have at least two bullet points to conform to proper style.

●●●

NOTE PowerPoint 2002 includes a rudimentary speech-recognition application, which allows you to speak commands (such and Enter and Delete), and PowerPoint carries them out. For now, this technology isn't particularly robust and takes more effort than it's worth for the short text you typically enter onto PowerPoint slides. However, if you want to explore it to enter your presentation contents, you have to install it separately because it's not installed with the typical installation of PowerPoint.

●●●

As you enter text, periodically save your file (BooksForEveryone 2). When you've entered all the text, save the file one more time, and go take a break. You've earned that second cup of coffee.

ON YOUR OWN: ENTERING TEXT IN AN OUTLINE

If you'd like to transfer what you've just practiced to your real-life presentation, simply follow these steps:

1. Open the PowerPoint file you saved with a title slide.

2. Click on the Normal view and click on the Outline tab.

3. With your cursor at the end of the last heading you typed, press Enter.

4. Type a new heading.

5. Promote the heading to make it the title of a new slide.

6. Press Enter and enter another heading, using the demote tool to make it a subheading of the new slide. Repeat this to enter all the bullet points for the presentation.

7. Continue entering text, using the promote and demote tools as you need to build your outline (or press Tab to demote and Shift+Tab to promote, if you prefer).

Organizing Your Thoughts

Most written material needs to be reworked several times before it's ready to be seen, and presentations are no exception. Now that you've created several slides in Normal view, you should take a step back from your content and look at it with an editor's eye. Is the information presented in a logical order? Do you need to add or delete information or even entire slides? PowerPoint makes it easy to do all of this and more.

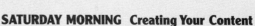

How to Build the Perfect Outline

People think differently, and Joe's method of building an outline doesn't necessarily work for Josephine. Some people prefer to enter all the main topic headings to establish the logical flow of topics and then go back and enter the detail points on each slide. Others prefer to build one complete slide after another. Either method works, as long as you have some logic to your final outline and have considered whether your audience can easily follow that logic.

Showing It All or Hiding Some Headings

Often, it's necessary to reorganize slides once you've created them to make the main points in your presentation flow more logically. Several tools in PowerPoint make that easy to do.

First, you can use the Collapse All tool on the Outline toolbar to remove detailed bullet points and display only slide headings, as in Figure 2.4. This allows you to view the higher-level organization of your slide.

You can also expand content one slide at a time, as shown in Figure 2.5. This is especially helpful in longer presentations when you want to focus on one or two slides at a time without the clutter of all the bullet points in your presentation on-screen.

TIP Note that you can expand one slide's outline on the Outline tab and then click on another slide to show its contents in the Slide Preview pane to its right. That lets you compare the detailed content of two slides, even if the slides are so far apart in the presentation that you couldn't possibly display them both on a single outline screen.

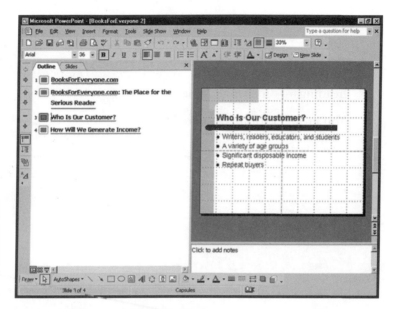

Figure 2.4

Collapsing the entire outline reveals the broad strokes of your presentation.

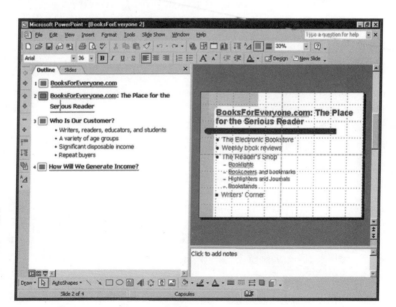

Figure 2.5

Slide 3 is opened in the outline, but Slide 2 is displayed in the slide preview on the right.

Creating a Summary Slide

Another way to get an overview of your presentation flow is to create a summary slide to list your major presentation ideas—that is, all the slide headings—on a single slide.

You create a summary slide by following these steps:

1. Display your presentation in Normal view.

2. Click on the Collapse All button to hide all bullet points on slides.

3. Click and drag to select all the slides in your outline.

4. Click the Summary Slide button on the Outline toolbar. A summary slide is inserted at the top of your outline, as shown in Figure 2.6.

Summary slides are useful either at the start or end of your presentation to give your audience a preview or wrap-up of key points. You can also review the summary slide to see how the flow of topic points works as you're editing. If you spot a problem, it's time to reorganize the content.

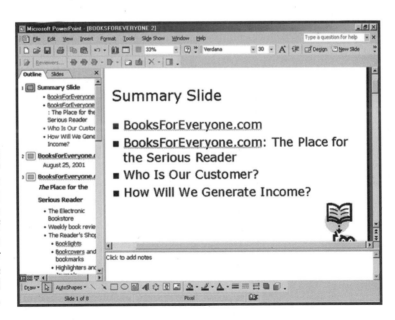

Figure 2.6

This instantly generated summary of the major points of your presentation helps you, and your audience, see the major points you'll be making.

Rearranging Your Outline

What if you find that you put the cart before the horse while drafting your presentation by putting your own ideas ahead of your boss's, a sure route to the unemployment line? No problem. You can easily move around items in a PowerPoint outline.

For example, you just inserted a summary slide for the presentation before the title slide. Your audience doesn't even know the name of your presentation, and you're already summarizing its content! It's a good idea to put a summary slide after a title slide. Try it:

1. Click on the slide to select it.

2. Click on the Move Down tool on the Outline toolbar. The summary slide now appears as the second slide in the presentation.

TIP

While working on reorganizing slides, you might want to enlarge the pane containing the Outline tab to be wider to make your text easier to read. Here's how: Place your mouse over the right-hand edge of the pane until the cursor turns into two lines with arrows pointing to either side. Click and drag the side of the pane to enlarge it.

What if you want to move a slide to a location 12 slides down in the outline? Do you click the Move Down button 12 times in a row? You could, but you've got better things to do with your time. If the location you want to move a slide to isn't so nearby, you might want to use a click and drag method.

Try the click-and-drag method now with a bullet point on Slide 3:

1. Click on the bullet point "Writers' Corner" to select it.

2. Without releasing the mouse button, drag the bullet point; as you do, a vertical line appears before headings to indicate that if you release the mouse at that point, that's where the text will appear.

NOTE If you are dragging a slide title to a new location rather than a bullet point, a dark horizontal line appears as you drag, indicating where the title will appear if you release your mouse.

3. When you reach the point where the vertical line is before the bullet point titled The Reader's Shop, release your mouse. Your presentation should now appear as shown in Figure 2.7.

4. Save your presentation.

TIP Are you a fan of cutting and pasting? If so, you'll be glad to know that you can always use those old standby editing functions anywhere in PowerPoint to move text from one place to another—even to another presentation using the Windows Clipboard.

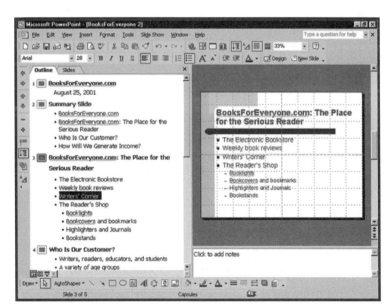

Figure 2.7

Moving headings around in Outline is a simple process.

Moving Slide Content to Different Levels

Okay, so let's get a little more complicated. What if you want to move a heading not only up or down in the outline, but you also want to change its level in the outline hierarchy? For example, what if you want to make a bullet point into the title of a new slide three slides back in the presentation? To make this move both in placement and hierarchy level, you have two choices:

- You can use the click-and-drag method to drag a bullet point from one slide to another. If you want to change the level of the item while moving it up or down in the outline, you must also drag it outward or inward on the outline before you release your mouse.

- If you want to use Move Up and Move Down buttons when you move a heading, it can only be moved to its current level in the outline. You must first change its level by demoting or promoting it and then move it up or down using the toolbar buttons or click-and-drag method.

Adding to Your Outline

Writing anything is a process of refining, and even Shakespeare probably threw away a few drafts of *Romeo and Janette* before he got it right. Part of this reworking process in a PowerPoint presentation is cutting out what's not relevant and adding details or topics that help your audience follow your train of thought and understand the points you want to make.

Adding a heading is simple: You simply place your cursor at the end of the bullet point that you want the new heading to follow and press Enter. If you want that text to move up or down a level in the outline, you can use the Promote and Demote tools.

You should be aware that if you place your cursor at the end of a slide title with the outline expanded and press Enter, you get a new slide title, but any bullet points that were under the existing slide title move down to become part of the new slide.

If you want to add a new slide title but you don't want to insert it under a bullet point and then promote it to become a new slide title, try this: Collapse the entire outline, place your cursor at the end of the slide title that will come before your new slide, and press Enter. The new item is inserted at the title slide level.

Sending a Slide Packing

To delete a slide, you simply select it by clicking on it and then press the Backspace or Delete key to remove it.

◆ ◆

Be sure you've selected the slide itself by clicking on the icon to its left in the outline or clicking on the slide itself in Slide Sorter view. If you select text on the slide and press Backspace or Delete, only the selected text will disappear, not the entire slide.

◆ ◆

Try adding and deleting text now in your sample presentation:

1. Select the first bullet point on the summary slide, BooksForEveryone.com. Because there's no need to include the title of the presentation as a bullet point in the summary slide, you'll get rid of it now.

2. Press Delete.

3. Page down to the last slide in the outline, and place your cursor at the end of the last bullet point, Strategic partnerships with book retailers.

4. Press Enter.

5. Click on the Promote button on the Outline toolbar. The heading is promoted to become the title of a new slide.

6. Enter the following text, and press Enter:
   How Will We Drive Traffic to Our Site?

7. Press Tab to move this next heading in one level.

8. Enter the following text (don't forget to press Enter at the end of each line to create a new bullet point):

   Targeted email campaign

   Advertising in selected print publications

   Strategic link generation and affiliate marketing program

9. Page up to display Slide 5 in the outline.

10. Select the bullet point Affiliate marketing and delete it.

11. Save the file.

Reorganizing Slide Order in Slide Sorter View

Some editing of your presentation involves adding and deleting content or moving headings around. Some involves organization at a higher level: moving entire slides around to create a better flow to your overall presentation.

Slide Sorter view is ideal for this, as well as for seeing the overall look and feel of your slides. In the sample presentation, we talk about how we'll generate income before we've explained how we're going to get people to come to the site. Let's flip that: First the people come, and then we get income!

1. Click on the Slide Sorter view button (in the lower-left corner of the screen). The Slide Sorter view appears, as shown in Figure 2.8.

2. Select the last slide by clicking on it. Notice that a selected slide has a thick black border around it.

3. Click and drag the slide to the left; a vertical black line appears, as shown in Figure 2.9.

4. When the horizontal line rests to the left of the slide titled How Will We Generate Income? release your mouse button. The slides are now in the proper order.

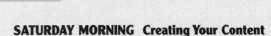

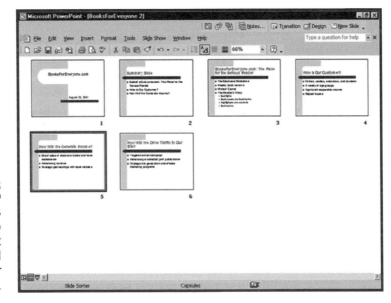

Figure 2.8

Slide Sorter view is a great place to reorganize content at the highest level of your presentation.

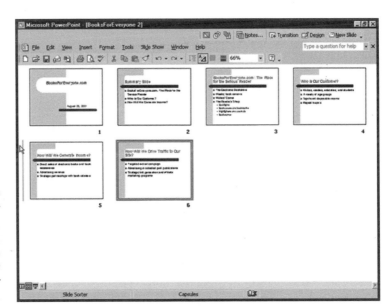

Figure 2.9

Your cursor changes into a hollow arrow, and a line appears to indicate new placement for your slide.

NOTE Using the click-and-drag method in Slide Sorter view, you can move one or more slides at a time. To move more than one contiguous slide (slides in the order they appear in the outline), select the first one, and then, holding down your Shift key, click the next one or more slides. If you want to move non-contiguous slides to a single new location, use the Ctrl key when selecting the slides. Then, use the click-and-drag method to move all the slides you've selected to a new location.

Duplicating Slides

Slide Sorter view is also the ideal place for duplicating slides. For example, if you'd like a summary slide at the beginning and end of your presentation, there's no need to create it twice. Create it once, duplicate it, and then move it where you want it to appear in your presentation. You might also want to build a new slide that has a lot of the same content as another slide; duplicating the first slide can save you some time.

TIP You can also use the traditional Copy and Paste commands to duplicate a slide. You have three ways to do this: use the Copy and Paste tools on the Standard toolbar; select these commands from the Edit menu; or use the shortcut keystrokes, Ctrl+C to copy and Ctrl+V to paste.

Try duplicating the summary slide you created earlier and moving it to the end of your presentation:

1. Click on the summary slide (Slide 2) to select it.

2. Select Insert, Duplicate Slide. The new slide appears to the right of the original.

3. Click and drag one of the summary slides to the end of the presentation.

4. Repeat the preceding process to duplicate the title slide and move it to the end of the presentation.

5. Save the file. Your presentation should now look like the one shown in Figure 2.10.

Deleting Slides

Okay, so we all make mistakes. I don't think we really need to repeat the title slide at the end of this presentation, so we'll just delete it. This, you'll be glad to hear, is simplicity itself:

1. Select the last slide in the presentation by clicking on it in Slide Sorter view.

2. Press Delete to get rid of it.

3. Save the file.

Now, go check on the children, your voicemail, or any leftovers from dinner last night. But come back in a little while to see how you get other people to do some of your work for you in PowerPoint.

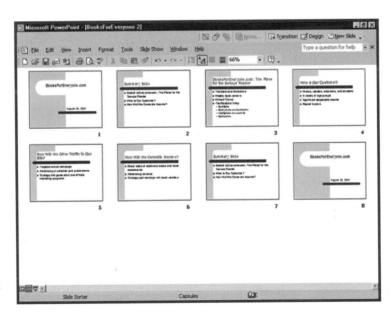

Figure 2.10

Your presentation is growing, and tools such as slide duplication make it easier!

ON YOUR OWN: EDITING PRESENTATION CONTENT

What's been covered since you last updated your own presentation is essentially the editing process. You must use your own powers of organization to see where you need to make changes or rearrange content to make a better flow in your presentation. Think of a presentation as you would any written document: Each paragraph (slide) should have a clear topic sentence (title), and each sentence in that paragraph (bullet point) should be relevant to the topic. If you have a run-on topic, you probably need to break information into more paragraphs (slides). Use the methods you learned in the preceding sections to make any needed edits in your presentation:

- Use Expand and Collapse tools to view what you need to see when reviewing your outline.

- Create a summary slide and place it after the title slide of your presentation to help you and your audience understand the broad organization of information.

- Use theOutline tab in the Normal view to move headings around and to add or delete headings.

- Use the Slide Sorter view to reorganize slides. Make a duplicate of your summary slide and move it to the end of your presentation.

Collaboration Tools

For this sample presentation, I can't supply you with sample co-workers. However, in your real-life presentations, you often interact with others in building polished presentations, so you need to know about PowerPoint's collaboration tools.

Over the life of your presentation, it's possible that several people will review your contents and make changes or comments. You might ask someone for help with design elements. And unless you work from a

cubicle on Mars, you probably will have meetings to discuss your presentation or its topic. PowerPoint offers powerful tools to streamline all of these collaboration efforts.

Email Collaboration

An easy way to get other people's comments or input on your presentation is to use email. Office XP is designed to make emailing presentations easy using Outlook or another email program.

Say that you've finished the first draft of your presentation on the viability of opening a branch office in Bora Bora, and you're ready to get some input. You want your boss to add some bullet points about salary levels, your marketing person to suggest some graphics that might make the presentation more effective, and your assistant to proof the presentation for errors. You could just attach the presentation to an email message, or use a feature PowerPoint offers to streamline your review process.

To send a PowerPoint presentation via email, follow these steps:

1. Start PowerPoint and open the presentation you want to send.

2. Select File, Send To, Mail Recipient (for Review).

3. Fill out addresses of recipients and any message (such as "Please get this back to me by Tuesday") in the email form that appears (see Figure 2.11).

4. Click on Send to deliver the message.

When the recipient opens the email and clicks on the attached presentation, it automatically opens in Slide Show view. The recipient can then right-click and select Speaker's Notes from the shortcut menu to add notes to each slide, save the presentation, and send it back to you as an attachment.

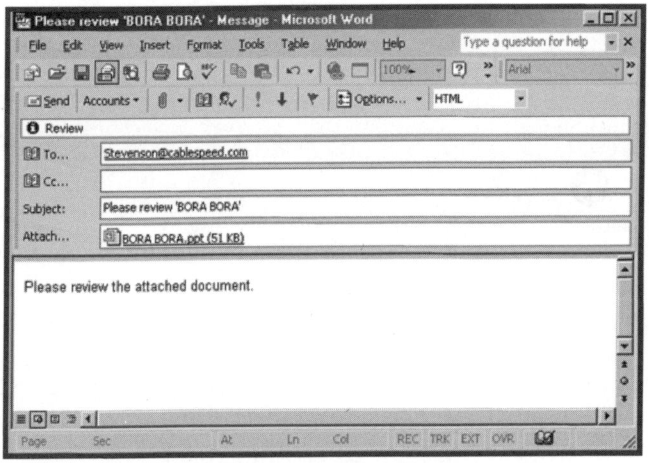

Figure 2.11

Although you can attach a PowerPoint presentation to any email program, sending a presentation through Outlook makes available some response tracking options.

Setting Up Team Sites

A great new collaboration feature in PowerPoint 2002 uses team sites. Team sites are Web sites that you and your colleagues or customers can use to share files, hold discussions, and post announcements or lists (such as team contact information). A team site, like the one shown in Figure 2.12, is really a command central for your presentation project.

Note that the server that you use to host a Team Site *must have Microsoft SharePoint,* a software product for collaborative learning environments, installed on it. If it doesn't, you won't be able to use this feature or follow the steps in this section. But Team Sites are such a powerful tool for collaboration, you might want to read on in any case to get an overview of their potential.

How Does a Team Site Work?

A team site is simply a Web site that you generate in minutes using FrontPage templates; FrontPage is Microsoft's Web design software, part of the Office suite of products. The site you create will look like the one in Figure 2.12, with discussion, event, and announcement areas already set up and areas for shared documents, contacts, and tasks, as well as a

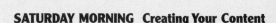
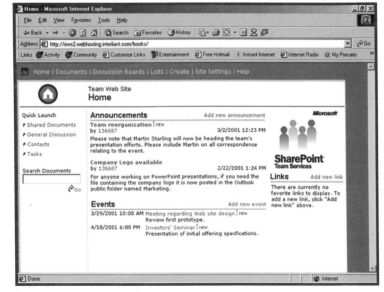

Figure 2.12

Share documents, discussions, events, and announcements at your own team site.

document search feature. Team sites can be hosted on an Internet or intranet (essentially an in-house Internet) server, such as Office Web Server or Microsoft Exchange Server 2000. Office Web Server comes with Office XP, although it isn't installed with the typical installation.

Creating a Team Site

To create a team site, you need to know a few things. First, you must have the URL of your Web server. (Your ISP or network administrator can provide this.) You should also have available a list of each of the people you want to access the team site:

To create your site, follow these steps:

1. With PowerPoint open, select File, New. The New Presentation pane appears.

2. Click on the Add Network Place item in this pane. The Add Network Place dialog box appears as shown in Figure 2.13.

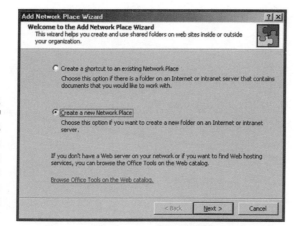

Figure 2.13

This dialog box lets you create either a shortcut to a network place, or a new folder on an Internet or intranet server.

3. Click on the Add Web Folder option and then on Open. The Add Network Place Wizard dialog box shown in Figure 2.14 appears.

NOTE

Steps 2 and 3 of the preceding procedure work this way if you have the Windows 2000 or Millennium operating system; if you have Windows NT 4.0 or Windows 98, you must click on Add Web Folder in the New Presentation pane and then Create a New Web Folder. Also, subsequent commands and dialog boxes in the wizard use the phrase "New Web" rather than "Network Place" in their names.

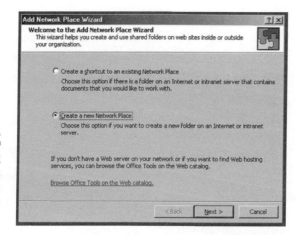

Figure 2.14

The Add Network Place Wizard guides you through creating your site step by step.

4. Select the Create a new Network Place option, and then click Next to proceed.

5. In the Add Network Place Wizard shown in Figure 2.15, enter the location on your network or the Internet where you want to create the site in the Folder location field. (Ask your network administrator to provide this URL if you're not sure; he or she may designate a folder for you to save the site in; if not, you should create or pick an existing folder for this step.)

6. Enter the name for the folder in the Folder Name field; for our sample presentation, you can use Books for Everyone, if you like, and press Next to proceed.

7. The dialog box shown in Figure 2.16 appears, requiring that you enter your User Name and Password. These should be supplied to you by your network administrator or whoever controls access rights to your intranet or Internet site. Enter both pieces of information, and click OK to continue.

8. The Add Network Place Wizard dialog box shown in Figure 2.17 appears. Here you designate the type of Web site you want to establish.

9. Click on SharePoint-based Team Web Site to select it, and then click on Finish to create the site.

Figure 2.15

The URL you enter here specifies the location on a server where you want the Web site to reside.

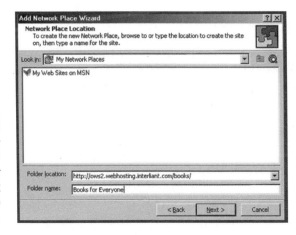

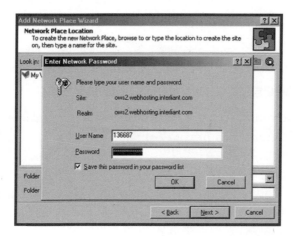

Figure 2.16

If you are placing a Web site on a server hosted by your ISP, ask it to provide you with this information.

When your site appears, it has the following features, shown in Figure 2.18:

- ○ A folder where you can post shared documents
- ○ A general discussion area where you can post comments to various discussion threads
- ○ Areas to post contact and task information
- ○ An announcement-posting area

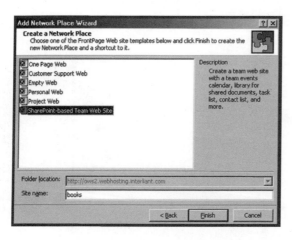

Figure 2.17

Each of these options is a FrontPage Web template, so generating a Web site is quick and easy.

○ An event-posting area

○ A listing area for favorite links

Establishing Roles

Now that you've set up a team site, you need to consider what kind of access you want each of your colleagues to have. For example, you might want your assistant and one co-worker to be able to get into the site and edit or add documents, but you want your boss to only read things on the team site, not change anything. You assign access rights by entering new user information and designating a role for each team member.

Follow these steps to add and make settings for a new user:

1. From the home page of the Web site, select Site Settings from the menu across the top of the page. The Site Settings page, shown in Figure 2.19, appears.

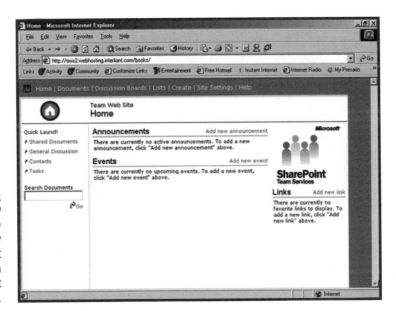

Figure 2.18

Everything is set up for you by Microsoft FrontPage, even a built-in document search feature.

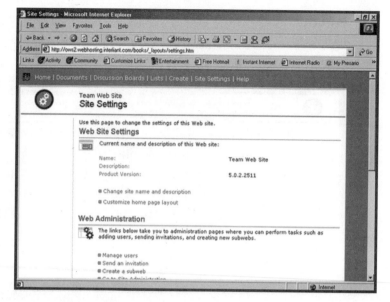

Figure 2.19

You can access several site settings from this one Web page.

2. Click on the Manage users link under the Web Administration area of this Web page. The Manage Users page appears (see Figure 2.20). Note that this page lists any users authorized to use the site (at this point, it should list only you) with user name and role. Also notice that as the creator of the site, you were automatically added and assigned the role of Administrator.

3. Click on the Add a user link to open the Add a User page shown in Figure 2.21.

4. With the Add a User page displayed, enter user information, including a User name entered when the person logs in to the site, password, and user or group name to help identify the user.

5. Select a User Role by simply checking one of the options presented here. Each choice provides a detailed list of actions each role is allowed to perform on the site.

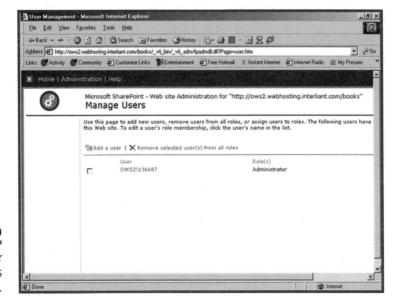

Figure 2.20

You can remove or add users from this page.

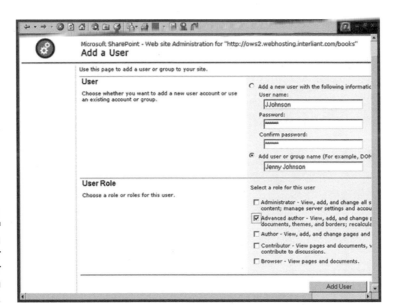

Figure 2.21

Here's where you designate a user and user role for your team members.

6. When you've entered user information and selected a role, click the Add User button to finish adding this user to your site.

You can go back to the Manage Users area at any time to modify a user's settings (by double-clicking on that user in the list of users), add new users, or delete a user.

Posting Announcements and Events

Posting announcements and events on the Team Web Site allows you to keep your team informed about issues and events related to your presentation project. Except for a slight difference in the information you fill out, these postings are created in a similar way.

To create an announcement, follow these steps:

1. Enter the Team Web Site URL in your browser window.

2. From the home page of the Team Web Site, click on Add new announcement. The Announcements: New Item form appears, as shown in Figure 2.22.

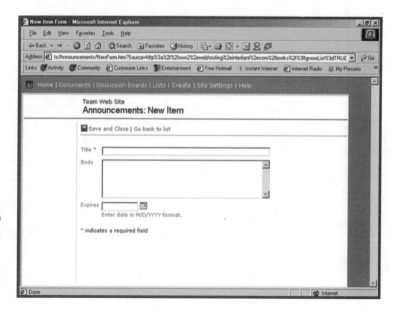

Figure 2.22

All you have to do to create an announcement is fill out this simple form.

3. Enter a title for the announcement.

4. Enter the announcement itself in the area labeled Body. Although you can enter just about as much information as you like, remember that it is displayed in its entirety on the home page, so be concise.

5. To indicate when the announcement should stop being displayed, enter a date in the Expires text box, or click on the calendar icon next to it and pick a date by clicking on it in the calendar month form that appears.

6. Click on Save and Close to post the announcement.

Entering an event is similar to the process you followed for announcements, except that you start by clicking on the Add new event link on the home page, and you fill out the information in the form shown in Figure 2.23.

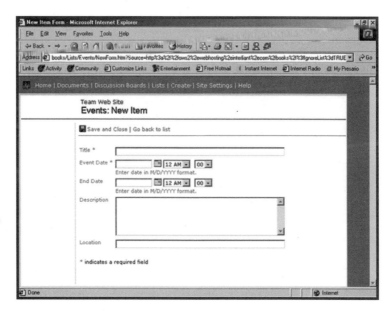

Figure 2.23

Events require a title, start and end date and time, a brief description, and a location.

When you've finished entering your announcement and event, your Team Web Site home page will look something like the one shown in Figure 2.24.

Posting PowerPoint Presentations to the Team Web Site

Often while working on a PowerPoint presentation, you'll want to make it or other documents related to it available to others in your organization. The Team Web Site provides a Shared Documents area that's perfect for this.

To place a PowerPoint presentation on the Team Web Site where it can be viewed and reviewed by others, you have to upload it to the Shared Documents page. To do so, follow these steps:

1. With the home page displayed, click on the Shared Documents link. The Shared Documents page shown in Figure 2.25 appears.

2. Click on the Upload Document link. The Shared Documents: Upload Document page appears, as shown in Figure 2.26.

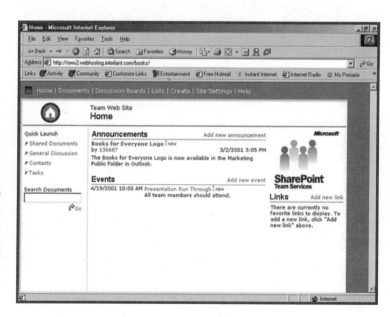

Figure 2.24

Your team members will spot important announcements and events every time they visit the Team Web Site.

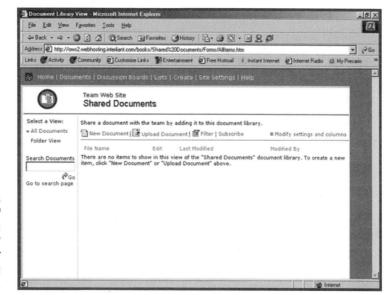

Figure 2.25

On this page, you can place new documents or upload existing ones.

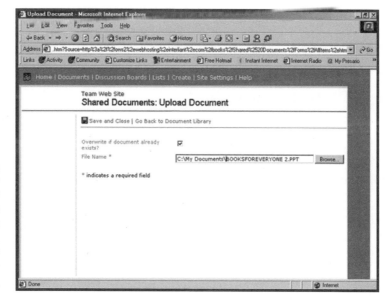

Figure 2.26

You can load any document you have access to, from your hard drive, floppy disk, or network, for example.

3. Enter the location and name of the file you want to upload, or click on the Browse button to locate it on your hard drive or network.

4. If you are comfortable overwriting any previously posted versions of the document with the same name, leave the check in the Overwrite if document already exists checkbox. If not, click to uncheck it.

5. Click on the Save and Close link to return to the Shared Documents page, where your document now appears.

Users looking for a shared document can open it by clicking on its link in this list.

Editing a Shared Document

If a team member clicks on the Edit icon next to a document in this list, the page shown in Figure 2.27 appears. This page allows a visitor to the site to delete a file, send it to someone else for review, start a discussion about it, or open it in PowerPoint and make changes. What you can do here depends on the role you are assigned and the access rights you have to modify Web site contents. After you make any changes, just save the file and it is saved on the Web site.

Notice that this page also includes a notation of when and by whom this file was last modified. This helps you keep track of the review cycle and who is making changes to your presentation through its various drafts.

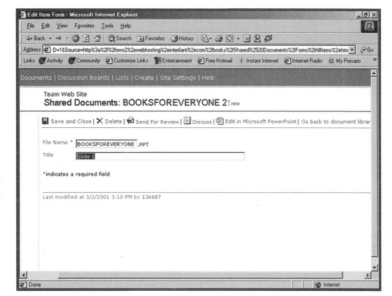

Figure 2.27

When you finish with a document, click on Save and Close to save any changes you made and return to the home page.

HOLDING ONLINE MEETINGS WITH NETMEETING

Although the discussion area in the Team Web Site is useful, sometimes you want to hold meetings in real time. This version of Office integrates Windows NetMeeting to make it easy to hold online meetings. NetMeeting makes both video and audio available to meeting participants, depending on each site's setup. When you're in an online meeting, you can make documents available to participants. A whiteboard feature lets participants make notes that are visible to all during the meeting. You can save both a transcript of the meeting and the contents of the whiteboard can be saved to print out for review at a later time.

Only a meeting host can send files to everybody at the meeting (that is, the person who initiated the meeting). If you host a NetMeeting, you can send a file using the File, Send To, Online Meeting Participant commands within Word, Excel, or PowerPoint.

What's Next?

Your presentation is really starting to take shape: You've built and reorganized your outline and even seen how you can work with others to review and revise it. Time for a lunch break. But when you come back, here's a rundown of what you'll do this afternoon:

- ✿ Work with design templates and slide layouts to add visual appeal to your presentation.
- ✿ Format text by working with fonts and adding various text effects.
- ✿ Learn the various options for previewing and printing a PowerPoint presentation.
- ✿ Use PowerPoint Masters to add elements to every slide quickly.

Have a nice lunch!

Working with Design

- ✿ Exploring presentation design basics
- ✿ Working with design templates and layouts
- ✿ Using PowerPoint masters
- ✿ Formatting text
- ✿ Adding notes to slides
- ✿ Printing a presentation

Presentation Design Basics

PowerPoint has plenty of built-in design tools to make building attractive presentations easy. Features such as design background templates, preset color schemes, and easy-to-insert graphics mean you don't have to be a graphic designer to make design part of your presentation agenda. However, having some design basics in your knowledge inventory will help you to orchestrate those design features more effectively.

Here are some things to keep in mind about presentation design:

- **Don't overdo.** Don't put too many graphics, too many words, too many animations, or too many font styles on a single slide. If you do, you might end up with a slide like the one in Figure 3.1.

- **Don't distract the listener from your message.** If the blinking purple logo in the corner of the slide distracts your audience from the content of your presentation, you should delete it.

- **Be consistent.** If you want to include your company Web site address on every slide, put it in the same place on every slide. (See information on using masters, later in this chapter, for help with this.) People watching a presentation should know where to look on each slide for a title, bullet points, and graphics so they don't have to hunt for information every time a new slide appears.

Figure 3.1

Overuse of graphics, mixing too many fonts on one page, and a wordy bullet point all make for presentation chaos.

✿ **Be conservative with multimedia.** If you want a flashy multimedia event, produce a music video. PowerPoint presentations are there to convey information, get a message across, or reinforce the speaker's content, not wow the audience with visual overload.

✿ **Special effects should punctuate, not overwhelm.** Use animations, sounds, elaborate transitions between slides, and even fancy text formatting only for occasional emphasis. Look for ways that these effects can support your message or help to break up presentation content for viewers, and avoid them when they simply create visual 'noise'.

Adding Pizzazz with Design Templates

PowerPoint has a few dozen design templates built into it. (You can also install additional templates from the Office CD or download them from Microsoft's Web site.) These templates can include background colors or patterns, graphic elements such as stars or illustrations, and text format-

ting and positioning on slides. By choosing one of these design templates for your presentation, you give it instant visual appeal.

On Friday night, you applied the Capsule design template. Now, you'll change to a different template and see how it affects the look and feel of your presentation:

1. Open the file you saved at the end of the last session. If you can't locate it, use the file from the CD titled BooksForEveryone 2.

2. Change to Slide Sorter view, if you aren't already displaying it. By displaying Slide Sorter view you'll be able to see how a new design affects all the slides in your presentation.

3. Select Format, Slide Design. The Slide Design pane appears to the right of your screen, as shown in Figure 3.2.

4. Scroll down in the list of templates that are available for use until you find the one called Crayons. (Note that to find a particular template, you hold your mouse over a design template preview and its name appears.)

You now have a few choices. You can simply click on the preview of the

Figure 3.2

Design, color, and animation templates all appear in the Slide Design pane.

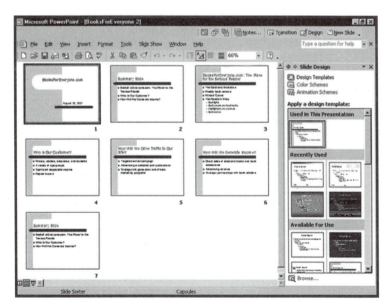

Crayons design template to apply it to the entire presentation. Alternately, you can click on the down arrow along the right side of the template preview. A short menu appears that allows you to Apply to All Slides or Apply to Selected Slides, which applies it to the slide appearing in Normal view or to multiple slides selected in Slide Sorter view.

NOTE

The ability to add design templates to individual slides, in effect, allowing you to use multiple designs in a single presentation, is new to PowerPoint 2002. This feature makes it possible for you to create a different visual mood for different sections of your presentation. But remember that consistency of look can help your audience to find information on slides easily and provides a tone to your presentation. If you vary design within one presentation, do so in a way that reinforces your message.

5. Click on the Crayon preview to apply the design to all slides in the presentation.

    Although the Crayon design template is fun and clean looking, it might be too childish to support the goal of the presentation to persuade investors to back a new Web business. You probably need a bit more conservative template. Because it's so easy to try on new designs, give it one more try.

6. Follow the preceding steps and apply the template named Pixel to the entire presentation.

7. Save the presentation with the name BooksForEveryone 3. Your presentation should now look like the one shown in Figure 3.3.

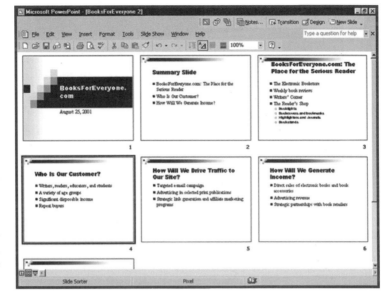

Figure 3.3

The ability to change the design template in an instant lets you try on different looks for your presentation.

Selecting Layouts

Layouts control the types of objects that appear on a slide and the positioning of those elements. Up to now, you've used only two layouts: title slide and text. By default, the first slide in a presentation uses a title slide layout with a title and subtitle; all other slides use the text layout, which consists of a slide title and bullet-point list.

◆ ◆

 **CAUTION**   You can insert objects other than those included in a layout onto a slide, but a layout gives you placeholders for objects that make them easier to work with. For example, when you click on a content object, PowerPoint provides six shortcuts to content objects you can use to instantly go to the source for that type of content, such as a spreadsheet or picture. Also, text you place on a page outside of layout objects does not show in the Normal view.

◆ ◆

Other layouts you can apply include elements such as pictures, charts or graphs, and multimedia objects. You can see some of the possible layouts by selecting Format, Slide Layout. The Slide Layout pane appears to the right of your presentation; I've enlarged this Slide Layout pane in Figure 3.4 to show you more layouts. Notice that some layouts place multiple items in a two-column arrangement.

TIP

The pane used for Layout, Slide Design and so on appears on the right side of your screen by default; this is its docked position. However, you can click and drag the pane so that it floats freely on your screen. If you do, when you next display it will be floating in the position where it appeared when you last displayed it.

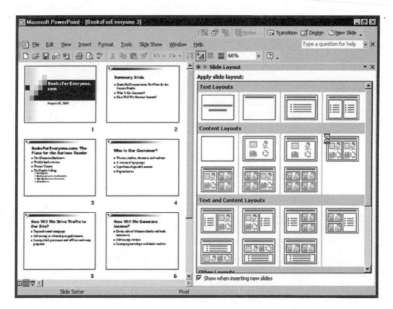

Figure 3.4

PowerPoint divides layouts into categories, such as text layouts and content layouts.

Applying a Layout to a Slide

You can apply a different layout to a slide on which you've already entered content or to a new slide. Try creating a new slide and applying a different layout to it:

1. With Normal view displayed, click on the next to last slide in the presentation outline to select it.

2. Select Insert, New Slide (or Ctrl+M). The new slide appears after the selected slide with the default text layout.

3. Select Format, Slide Layout to display the Slide Layout pane.

4. Scroll down in the Slide Layout previews until you find the layout called Text & Content. (The name of the layout appears when you hold your mouse over its preview.)

5. Click on the arrow along the right edge of the layout preview and select Apply to Selected Slides from the drop-down menu that appears.

6. Close the Slide Layout pane by clicking on the Close button in the upper-right corner.

7. Save the presentation.

Your new slide should look like the one in Figure 3.5.

Editing Objects on the Slide Layout

Up to now, you've entered all content for the presentation in Normal view. However, you can also enter content using the placeholders a layout provides on individual slides. You'll insert some of the content objects for this slide in the next session. For now, you'll enter text using placeholders on this slide:

1. Click on the title object; the placeholder text disappears and a blinking insertion point appears, ready for you to enter text.

2. Type this title: **Projected Five Year ROI** (ROI stands for return on investment).

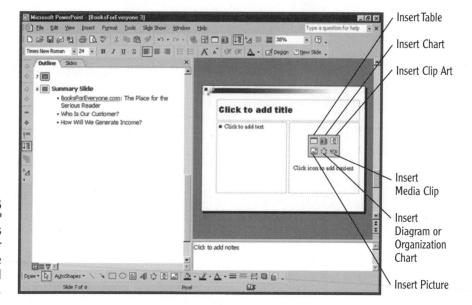

Insert Table

Insert Chart

Insert Clip Art

Insert Media Clip

Insert Diagram or Organization Chart

Insert Picture

Figure 3.5

This layout has three placeholder objects: a slide title, bullet list, and content.

3. Click on the text object beneath the title; this is where bullet points appear. Again, the placeholder text disappears and the object is ready for entering text.

4. Type these three bullet points, pressing Enter after each one: **Funding level of $2.5 million; Expected yearly profits of $750,000; Return on investment year five, $1.25 million.**

5. Save the file.

Your slide should now look like the one shown in Figure 3.6.

Mastering PowerPoint Masters

As easy as it is to make design and formatting changes in PowerPoint, it can get tedious when you have a presentation with dozens of slides. Changing the font of every title object or adding your company logo to each and every slide is right up there with having a root canal.

Luckily, PowerPoint has provided an easy-to-use feature to save you the trouble. It's called *masters*. Use masters to make global changes, such as

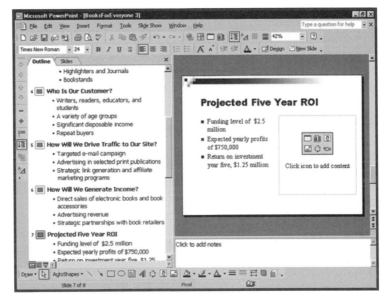

Figure 3.6

Placeholder objects make entering text simple; notice each text object contains its own text formatting determined by the slide design and layout.

placing a company logo on every slide or changing the font or position of all the titles for your slides. The three kinds of masters all store specifications for the design template, including font, bullet-list styles, background color and design, and placeholders for objects. You can add anything you like to a master, such as text or graphics you want to appear universally in your presentation.

Here's what the three masters are used for:

You use *Slide Master* to make global changes to the title slide and content slides in a presentation, such as modifying the font for all titles or bullet points, changing the positioning of the title placeholder, or adding a company logo.

TIP

Note that you can override global background changes on individual slides, which you do by selecting a slide in any view, selecting Format, Background, and checking the Omit Background Graphics from Master checkbox.

Handout Master helps you add elements to printed audience handouts, such as adding your phone number to each page so that people can call you with questions after the presentation.

When you print a presentation, you can print it with an area for notes displayed, as shown in Figure 3.7. You might want to use *Notes Master* to include a brief outline of the presentation to help you keep your place during your talk, for example. Notes Master allows you to add elements to every page when you print a notes version of your presentation.

No matter which master you use, adding things to each works pretty much the same.

Using Masters

You make changes to any of the three types of masters by displaying the appropriate master view and then inserting objects, moving placeholders, or making any of the formatting changes you've learned about in this session.

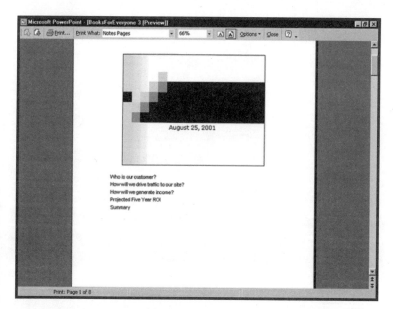

Figure 3.7

Notes can help a speaker keep his place or provide backup information on the points in each slide.

CAUTION Masters are the place for global changes or text such as presentation date; you do not enter the text for your presentation here. Specific presentation text is added on individual slides.

When you work with Slide Master, you actually work with a pair of masters called the slide-title master pair. One of these controls the presentation's title slide and is called the title master and one controls all the other slides in the presentation and is called the slide master. One reason for this is that many times you'll want to omit items included in the body of the presentation, such as slide number, from the title slide in the presentation.

CAUTION Frankly, the terminology used here is a bit confusing, because the feature you use to control masters is the Slide Master, and one of the pair of masters within that feature is called the slide master. I'll differentiate between them here by capitalizing the feature name.

To display the Slide Master, follow these steps:

1. Open your PowerPoint presentation, which you saved earlier.
2. Select View, Master, Slide Master. The Slide Master view appears, as shown in Figure 3.8.

Note that a pair of masters appears to the left: one is the title master and one is the slide master. Also, the Master view contains its own floating toolbar. Notice also the three placeholders along the bottom for footer text. You might use footer text to include the date of the presentation, the name of the presenter, a department name, or a slide number, for example.

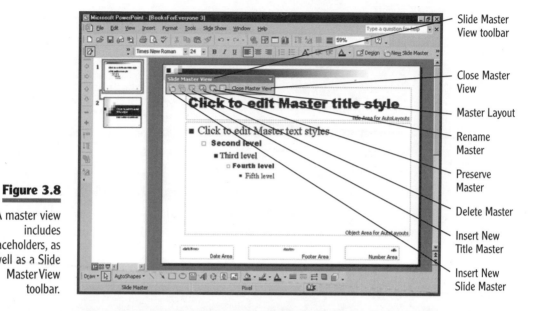

Slide Master
View toolbar

Close Master
View

Master Layout

Rename
Master

Preserve
Master

Delete Master

Insert New
Title Master

Insert New
Slide Master

Figure 3.8

A master view
includes
placeholders, as
well as a Slide
Master View
toolbar.

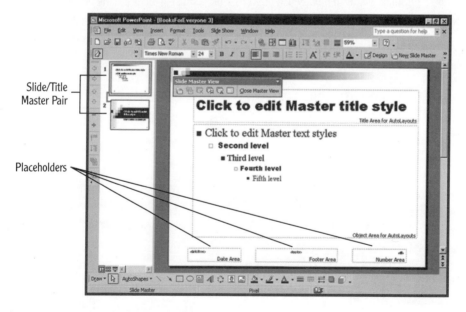

Slide/Title
Master Pair

Placeholders

Here are some rules of thumb for how masters work:

✿ If you change a title object on the slide master, all slide titles in the presentation that use that master are affected. The title on the title slide, however, is not changed, because that is controlled by the title master.

✿ Footer information added to the slide master won't appear on the title slide and vice versa.

✿ If you want to change subtitle style, you must display the title master because that's the master that contains the subtitle placeholder; if you want to change bullet-list style, you must display the slide master where the bullet-list placeholder appears.

✿ The bullet-list placeholder allows you to make global changes level by level in the outline; the slide master provides placeholders for up to five levels of bullet points. Make changes to the placeholder for one level, and all headings at that level in the presentation take on that formatting.

✿ If you make changes to individual slides, those changes will override slide-title master settings, but master settings will not override individual slide settings. For that reason it is best to apply master settings early in your design process before you do any formatting on individual slides.

Now that you have the Slide Master view displayed, make a change to the first level of bullet points:

1. If the title master is displayed, click on the slide master.

2. Click on the bullet-list placeholder; the first level of bullets is highlighted, ready for editing.

3. Click the arrow on the right side of the Font drop-down list to open it.

4. Scroll down to the font named Verdana, or a similar sans serif font, and click on it to apply it.

5. Save the presentation.

Now every first level bullet in the presentation will use the Verdana font, unless you override an object on an individual slide or apply another master to it.

TIP

Bullets and numbering that are applied automatically do not change font when you format text. You have to go to the bullets and numbering dialog box through the Formatting menu to make changes to these.

Working with Multiple Masters

If you use more than one design template in a presentation (which you can do by inserting a new slide master from master view or applying more than one Slide Design to selected slides in your presentation), you end up with multiple versions of masters. All the masters are displayed along the left side of the Master view as shown in Figure 3.9, and you can click on any one of them to display it and make changes.

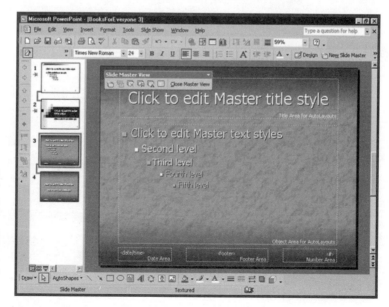

Figure 3.9

You might have several sets of masters if you've applied several design templates throughout your presentation.

When you have created multiple masters, you can no longer make a change to all slides in your presentation on one master; you must make changes to each master or set of slide-title masters. The Master toolbar gives you control over multiple masters with the following tools:

- Create new masters by using the Insert New Slide Master or Insert Title Slide Master. This will be a custom master that you can design as you please (in other words, it doesn't use a built-in slide design). You can also insert a new slide-title master pair by displaying the Slide Design pane while in Master View and selecting a new slide design.

- Use the Delete Master tool to delete a master.

- If you do not apply a particular slide-title master pair to any slides in your presentation, PowerPoint might delete that pair. To ensure that that doesn't happen, select the master and click the Preserve tool on the Master toolbar.

- Use the Rename tool to rename a slide-title master pair.

- You can use the Master Layout tool to redisplay any type of place-holder you may have deleted from a master.

Adding Graphics

Although you'll be working more with graphics tomorrow morning, right now you need to see how inserting a graphic on a master adds it to the entire presentation, so you'll insert a piece of clip art. Clip art is a collection of drawings and illustrations that comes with Office XP.

◆ ◆

It's important that when you place a graphic object on a master, you also size it to work well with your layout and place it in a location where it's not likely to interfere with text, such as where a longer bullet point might run over it. You'll learn about resizing graphics in tomorrow's session.

◆ ◆

Follow these steps to place a piece of clip art on your slide master:

1. With slide master displayed, select Insert, Picture, Clip Art. The Clip Art pane shown in Figure 3.10 appears on the right side of your screen.

NOTE   If you haven't used the Clip Art feature before, an Add Clips to Organizer Now/Later/Options dialog box will appear at this point. If you have never used the Clip Art feature, there will also be no search term in the Clip Art dialog box; if you have, the last search term you used appears there.

2. Click in the Search text box and delete the term that appears there.

3. Enter the search word **books,** and click on the Search button. The results of the search appear with previews of relevant clip art.

4. Click on the arrow along the side of the second choice. (If your choices differ slightly, choose a similar piece of art.) A drop-down menu appears, as shown in Figure 3.11.

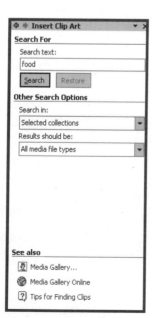

Figure 3.10

You can search for illustrations by keyword or even get images from the Web.

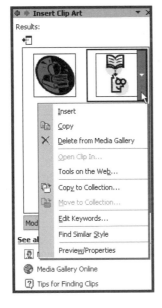

Figure 3.11

You'll learn more about the Clip Art menu tomorrow; for now, all you have to do to place a picture is select Insert.

5. Select Insert from the menu. The clip art appears on the master slide, and a Picture toolbar appears, as shown in Figure 3.12.

6. Click on the clip art object and drag it to the bottom-right corner of the slide master.

As you'll see shortly, you've just placed this graphic on every slide in your presentation, except the title slide.

Adding Global Text

One great use of masters is to add global text; that is, text that you want to appear on every slide in your presentation. You can use global text for a variety of reasons:

✿ Add a draft number as you're working on a presentation so all collaborators can keep track of the version.

✿ Add the date of the presentation.

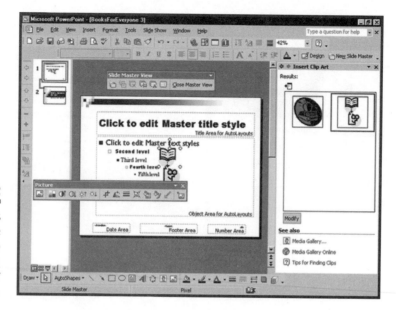

Figure 3.12

The image appears in the middle of the slide; you have to move it where you want it to appear on all slides.

⚙ Place your company name on each slide.

⚙ Add a slide number to each slide to help you reference a slide for the audience as they review their handouts.

You'll add a date to your sample presentation now:

1. On the non-title slide master, click in the Date Area footer to open it for editing.

2. Highlight the current text (date/time).

3. Type this date: **August 25, 2001**.

4. Click anywhere outside of the date area.

5. Save the file.

Now it's time to see what your changes to the master have done to your presentation in Print Preview. Click the Close Master View item on the Master toolbar. Your presentation should look like the one in Figure 3.13.

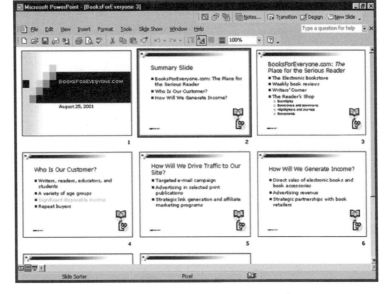

Figure 3.13

A date appears in the left-bottom corner of every slide and a graphic in the right.

Formatting Text

Obviously in the work you've done so far on the sample presentation, somebody applied formatting to your text. That was PowerPoint. It applies certain text formats from the design template you choose and other formats, such as text size and boldness, depending on the type of text object. (For example, title objects are typically bolder and use a larger font size than bullet items in a text object.)

But you don't have to leave your text formatting at the default settings. You can explore the range of text formatting options available to you to add distinctiveness to your presentations.

Before you begin, I want to emphasize one basic concept about formatting text in PowerPoint: Your first goal should always be readability. If you choose a fancy font that looks good but isn't legible from the fourth row of the meeting room, you might as well phone in your presentation.

Understanding Fonts

The odds are you've dealt with fonts before in working with your word processor program or other desktop applications. A font is simply a style for type. There are script fonts, symbol fonts that contain little pictures or symbols, and mathematical fonts, for example.

The fonts you'll work with for the most part when dealing with the words in your presentation fall into two style categories: serif and sans serif. Serif refers to the little backward lines, known as feet, that come off the tops or bottoms of some letters, such as l, p, and r. Fonts such as Times New Roman include these tiny lines. Fonts such as Arial don't; they're sans serif fonts (sans means "without", in case you missed French class in high school). Figure 3.14 shows three serif fonts, followed by three sans serif fonts.

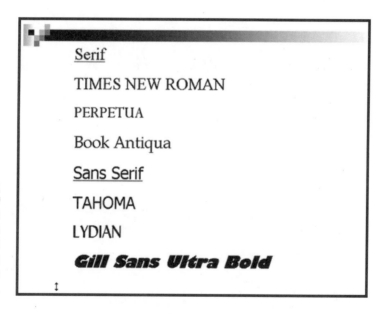

Figure 3.14

The last three fonts on this slide are sans serif, the font type that works best in headings and presentations.

One rule of thumb is that serif fonts work better for lengthier pieces of text because they help the reader's eye move from one character to the next; that's why many books are set in a serif font. Sans serif fonts are often used for newspaper or magazine headlines; because they don't have those little flags as bridges to the next letter, they tend to stop the eye and help it focus on a short message. Generally, sans serif fonts work better in slide presentations.

NOTE •
Did you know some fonts were designed to be viewed online? Most of these fonts, such as Verdana and Tahoma, have clean open styles that work well when read on-screen. If your presentation will be viewed on a computer screen or projected from a computer, consider this in selecting your fonts.
• •

Applying a Font

You can apply a font to a single character, word, title, bullet point, or all the text in your presentation. It's simply a process of selecting the text you want to format and then selecting a font from the font drop-down list on the Formatting toolbar. However, if you want to make any global font changes, such as having all headings or bullet points appear in a different font, you should make those changes on the Master. Remember, changes to individual slides will override Master settings.

CAUTION ◆
You shouldn't use more than three or four fonts in your entire presentation to avoid a cluttered, inconsistent look.
◆ ◆

Follow these steps to change the font in your sample presentation:

1. Display the Slide Master.

2. Click on the slide master to display it.

3. Click on the Title object and press Escape.

4. Click on the arrow next to the Font drop-down list to open it. The most recently used fonts appear at the top of the list, followed by an alphabetical list of all available fonts, as shown in Figure 3.15.

5. Using the scrollbar to the right of this list, locate the font named Verdana, a contemporary looking sans serif font, and click on it. The title object on the slide master will now be formatted in the Verdana font.

6. Repeat the steps above with the bullet-point object on the slide master. When you've finished all the text in your presentation has been changed to Verdana.

7. Now click on the title master to display it.

8. Click on the title object and press Escape.

9. Open the Font drop-down list and scroll to locate the font called Copperplate Gothic Light. This elegant serif font adds a touch of distinction to the presentation title.

10. Click on the font name to apply it. Your first slide should now look like the one shown in Figure 3.16.

11. Save the file.

Figure 3.15

The Font menu shows you a sample of how each font looks.

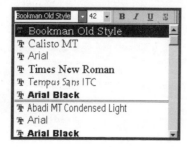

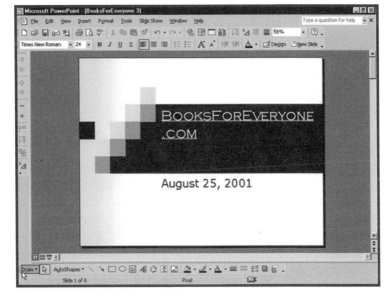

Figure 3.16

Notice how the different font style makes the presentation title stand out.

Changing Font Size

Another logical change you might want to make to text in your presentation is to adjust the size. Although PowerPoint sets text at a logical size for each object, and even has a feature called AutoFit that adjusts the sizing based on the length of an object (for example, if you have three bullet points, they are a larger font size than six bullet points), sometimes you have to take control.

TIP You can turn off AutoFit by deselecting that option in the AutoCorrect Options dialog box, which you can display from the Tools menu.

Look at the title slide for a moment. There's a slight problem with the way the presentation title fits on the page: It breaks at an awkward place, pushing the .com portion to the second line. One way to get all that text to fit on one line is to resize it.

NOTE Other ways to get text to fit on a single line are to widen the text object by selecting it and dragging on the round white handles on the right or left side of it; to try a different slide design that provides a wider area for text; or to place your cursor at a more logical point for the line to break and press Shift+Enter.

Correct that text problem now by changing the font size:

1. Click and drag to select the title.
2. Click on the Font Size drop-down list arrow to display it.
3. Scroll down and click on 32. This applies a 32-point font size to the text.
4. Click on the subtitle object containing the date; typically, the title of a presentation should be larger than the subtitle, so modify this text as well.
5. Press Esc to go into editing mode for the text in the subtitle object.
6. Open the Font Size drop-down list and change the size of this text to 28 points.
7. Save the presentation.

Your title slide should now look like the one in Figure 3.17.

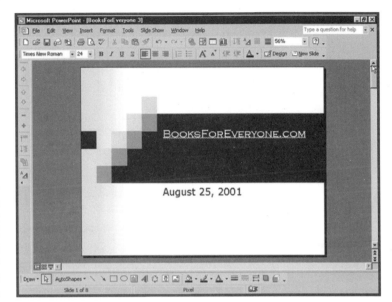

Figure 3.17

Generally, the text of a heading should be a bit larger than the subheading for emphasis, as in this slide.

Working with Text Effects

Applying a font and adjusting font size are two basic ways to change the look of text on your slides. But other tools available help to add emphasis, such as bold, italic, and underline effects. In addition, you can change the color of your text; you might do that to make it stand out more, to make it match your company colors, or to highlight certain text.

Making Text Bold, Italic, or Underlined

The three text effects of bold, italic, and underline are good for emphasizing a particular word in a text object, but remember, they don't usually work on a large amount of text. A presentation that uses bold or italic text throughout, for example, is typically not that easy to read.

Applying these effects is as easy as selecting text and clicking on the Bold, Italic, or Underline tool button on the Formatting toolbar. Try changing a word in the presentation to italic:

1. Use the scrollbar to display the third slide, which is titled BooksForEveryone.com: The Place for the Serious Reader.

2. Click on the title object to open it for editing.

3. Select the word The following the colon.

4. Click the Italic tool button to format it.

5. Save the presentation.

Now you have added emphasis to the phrase, suggesting that BooksForEveryone.com is the *one and only* place for the serious reader!

Working with Text Color

You can make text any color of the rainbow, from a scintillating pink to a murky green. You can change font color letter-by-letter or throughout an entire presentation. As with every other design effect, text color should be used judiciously.

Whether you're using color as an accent to highlight a piece of information or changing the color of all the text in your presentation, always choose a font color that is in strong contrast to the slide background color, such as a yellow font on a black background. This greatly enhances the readability of text.

To change font color, follow these steps:

1. Using the scrollbar to the right of the slide pane, scroll down to display Slide 4, which is titled Who Is Our Customer?

2. Click on the text object to open it for editing.

3. Click and drag to select the bullet point, Significant disposable income.

4. Click on the arrow on the right side of the Font Color tool on the Formatting toolbar.

5. Select More Colors. The Colors dialog box appears.

6. Click on a color in the Standard color palette, such as a red, blue, or green that will contrast with the white background of the presentation; a preview appears, as shown in Figure 3.18.

7. Click OK to apply the selected color. The dialog box disappears, and you return to the slide.

Click anywhere outside the selected text object to see how the new color looks.

TIP If you want even more color choices, you can use the Custom tab of the Colors dialog box to specify unique values of red, green, and blue. By designating color values with this system, you can designate millions of shades. Many companies use this system to more closely match corporate logos colors, for example.

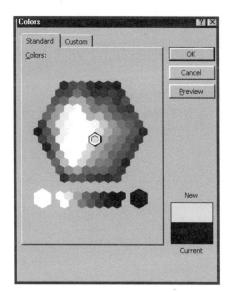

Figure 3.18

You can choose from a wide range of colors or ranges of gray between black and white.

ON YOUR OWN

Time to apply all you've just learned to that presentation your boss wants Tuesday morning. Follow these steps to bring your own presentation up to speed:

✿ Change your design template: Select Format, Slide Design to display the Slide Design pane. Click on Design Templates to display template previews, and then click on a preview to apply a design template to your presentation.

✿ Change slide layout: Select Format, Slide Layout. Click on the arrow along the side of a layout preview you want to use, and then select Apply to Selected Slides to apply it to the slide currently displayed in the slide pane.

✿ Enter additional text for slides directly on the slides themselves by clicking on text objects to select them and then entering or editing the text there.

✿ Apply formatting to text: Display the Slide Master. Then use the Font, Font Size, or Font Color tools on the Formatting toolbar to make new choices from drop-down lists. You can also click on the Bold, Italic, or Underline tool buttons to add these effects to selected text.

✿ If you want to make changes to formatting on specific slides, display those slides in Normal view, select objects and make the changes. Just remember that any changes made here override Slide Master settings.

Taking a Break

If you've come this far, you're really getting the hang of doing things in PowerPoint, so you should feel a sense of accomplishment. However, I'm sure you can think of better things to be doing on a Saturday afternoon— so go do one of them—a short one. Come back ready to tackle a couple of more challenges before you quit for the evening.

Adding Notes to Slides

I don't know about you, but when I make a presentation, I like to have close at hand all the facts and figures to back up my assertions. Once I used index cards, but after more paper cuts than I care to remember and a few out-of-sequence faux pas, I switched to using PowerPoint notes.

Notes added to a slide in your presentation appear beneath the slide image when you print the notes version of your presentation. Adding a note is a simple process:

1. Display Slide 7 in the presentation, titled Projected Five Year ROI.
2. Click near the bottom of the screen, in the box that says "Click to add notes."
3. Type this note: **Figures based on total yearly income of $1.8 million.**

That's it: You'll see the results of this entry when we look at a notes print-out later in the chapter (Figure 3.25 if you want to peek ahead!).

Printing Your Presentation

Presentations don't typically reside only in your computer or projected on an overhead display. Throughout the drafting of your presentation, you'll probably need to print it out to do some editing of your ideas on paper prior to implementing them in PowerPoint or to circulate it for review. Also, it's advisable to print out audience handouts of the contents of the presentation; you can give these out before your presentation so your listeners can follow along and even make notes, or provide them after the presentation so that they have a reference to look at later to remember your ideas if you feel they might distract your listeners during the presentation. Finally, as the presenter, you might benefit from a printed version of your slides, along with any notes that help you remember important points or back up data as you speak.

PowerPoint lets you print four things:

- ✿ The outline of your presentation
- ✿ The slides from your presentation
- ✿ Audience handouts with space for notes
- ✿ Speaker notes that include slides and notes you've added to slides

Using Print Preview

Print Preview allows you to see your presentation exactly as it should appear when you print it on paper. Preview allows you to spot problems—perhaps with a misspelled word you missed or the way a lengthier bullet point breaks on a line—before you spend time and paper printing.

NOTE   If you've used previous versions of PowerPoint, you might be aware that it had no Print Preview feature. I assume Microsoft figured that by running a slide show on-screen, you could get the sense of how a printed version would look. But most people are accustomed to seeing print previews in other software programs, and they come in handy for showing you how handouts and notes versions of slides will appear on a printed page.

With a presentation open, all you have to do to display Print Preview is to click on the Print Preview tool button on the Standard toolbar, or display the Print dialog box and click on the Preview button. Figure 3.19 shows one slide in this presentation in Print Preview mode with the Options menu displayed. Notice the object you placed on the slide master; it appears on every slide but the title slide, along with the date.

Previous Page
Next Page
Print
Print What

Help
Close
Options
Portrait
Landscape
Zoom

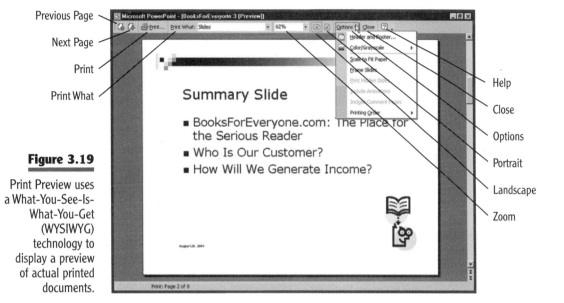

Figure 3.19

Print Preview uses a What-You-See-Is-What-You-Get (WYSIWYG) technology to display a preview of actual printed documents.

NOTE

To preview a Web presentation, you select File, Web Page preview to display it in your Web browser.

The choices on the Print Preview toolbar (see Figure 3.19) allow you to navigate your presentation in preview or control how your document prints:

🔧 Previous Page moves you one page back in the presentation, and Next Page moves you forward.

🔧 Print sends the document to the printer, and Print What allows you to select whether to print an outline, slides, notes, or handouts.

🔧 Zoom allows you to make the Preview larger or smaller or fit it exactly on the full page.

🔧 Portrait and Landscape let you display the printed Notes or Handout page with the 8 1/2-inch side of the paper along the top and bottom or along the left and right. (See Figure 3.20.)

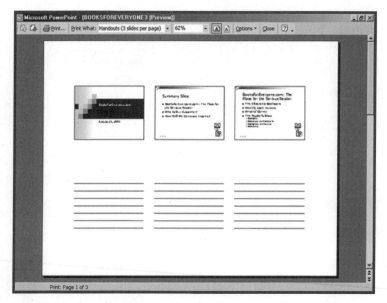

Figure 3.20

Here's a handout printed with landscape orientation.

The choices on the Options menu provide even more control over how your document prints:

☼ Color/Grayscale allows you to control how a black and white version of a presentation prints. You can print a Color presentation on a black and white printer. Use Grayscale to show shades of gray representing variations in color, or Pure Black and White, which shows no gradations of gray.

☼ Scale to Fit Paper lets PowerPoint adjust the positioning of slide contents to fit all contents on the printed page.

☼ Frame Slides places a thin-line frame around each slide on the page, as in Figure 3.21. This looks better with some design templates than others!

☼ The next three commands on this menu control what prints. You can include slides you've hidden in your on-screen presentation with the Slide Show, Hide Slide command by selecting the Print Hidden Slides option; you can also choose to include comments pages in a printout.

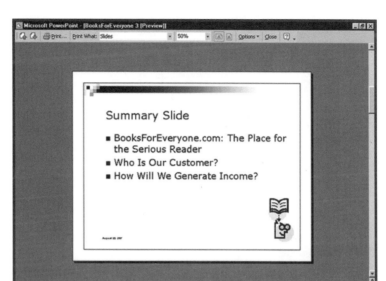

Figure 3.21

The frame around each slide can create a helpful visual boundary for each element of your presentation.

⚙ Finally, you can control the order in which pages print. This setting affects only handouts, where you can print multiple slides on a single page. If you choose a six-slides-per-page printout, for example, you can print them horizontally (Slide 1 in the upper-left corner, Slide 2 in the upper-right corner, Slide 3 below Slide 1 on the left, and so on) or vertically (Slide 1 in the upper-left corner, Slide 3 to the right of it, Slide 2 below Slide 1, and so on). Figure 3.22 shows a preview of a handout with six slides to the page, displayed horizontally. Most people feel more comfortable with the horizontal display because it reads left to right across the page as a line of text does.

After you've made selections in Print Preview, you can print by simply clicking on the Print button on the toolbar. Because you made most of your choices with tools in Print Preview, no Print dialog box appears. For now, click on the Close button to close Print Preview.

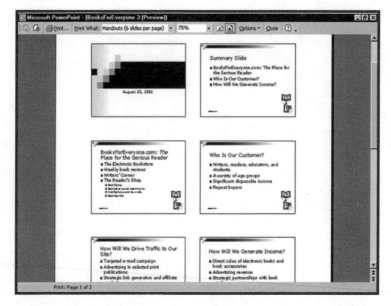

Figure 3.22

You read this presentation from the left side of the page to the right, then back to the left side of the next line of slides, and so on.

 TIP If you want to make changes to where a presentation prints (to a specific printer or to a file that you can email to a co-worker or send to a slide company to generate slides) or how many copies to print, or you want to print only a range of slides, you have to use the Print dialog box.

Using the Print Dialog Box

Many of the options available in Print Preview are also available in the Print dialog box, which is shown in Figure 3.23. You display this dialog box by selecting File, Print.

The following list outlines things you can control from here, in addition to those settings described in the Print Preview section earlier:

✿ **Printer:** Here you can designate a wealth of information about where you want your presentation to print. You can print to any standard printer, faxing software, or a file. The printer you designate as your default printer in Windows appears in the Name field

Figure 3.23

You can control every detail of your presentation output from this dialog box.

when you open the Print dialog box. You can choose other printers from the Name drop-down list. You must have added a printer through the Windows Start menu (Start, Settings, Printer) for it to be available in the Name drop-down list.

TIP

If you want to get actual slides (not paper ones), you should save your presentation and then send the file to a slide company. If you email your file, many companies can generate slides and ship them to you the following day.

✿ **Print Range:** You can print only selected slides in Slide Sorter view, the currently displayed slide in Normal view, or a designated range of slides (such as 3-10).

✿ **Number of Copies:** Here you enter a number of copies to print (use the up and down arrows in this field to change this setting) and check the checkbox to collate copies.

NOTE

If you want to print a presentation on a color printer, you need to designate that printer in the Print dialog box, but you also need to set up your presentation to print in color by selecting View, Color/Grayscale, Color before you print.

Controlling Printer Properties

When you designate a printer in the Print dialog box, you can also control the printer properties by clicking on the Properties button in the top of the Print dialog box. The Properties dialog box appears, as shown in Figure 3.24. Depending on your type of printer, you may see different settings available here.

Between you and me, I could go into exhaustive detail about every choice on the four tabs of this dialog box, but you won't ever use most of them. For that reason, and because you want to get a presentation done in a weekend, here are the settings you're likely to need:

✿ **Paper Size:** Are you using 8 $1/2$ X 11 paper or legal paper (8 $1/2$ X 14)? Control that here, or create a custom paper size with the Custom option.

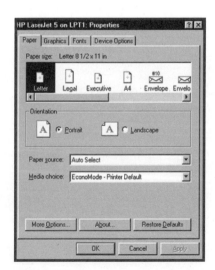

Figure 3.24

Control the size of paper, graphics, fonts, and print quality from here.

❂ **Orientation:** Landscape is the usual choice for slides, but if you want your slides to print in the direction of a typical business letter, change to Portrait here.

❂ **Paper Source:** If you are sending to a printer that holds stationery in one tray and plain paper in another, and perhaps even transparency stock in a third, pick your paper tray source here.

❂ **More Options:** If you'd like to print on two sides of a piece of paper and your printer supports this, click the More Options button on the Paper tab.

❂ **Graphics:** Click the Graphics tab to control the resolution (dots per inch) and the intensity (darkness) of your printout.

Click OK to close the Properties dialog box without making any changes and return to the Print dialog box.

Print What?

As I said earlier, you can print four versions of your PowerPoint presentation: the Normal view, slides, notes pages, or handouts. You choose what to print by selecting it from the Print What drop-down list in the bottom-left corner of the Print dialog box.

Slides prints one slide per page; Normal view prints the presentation outline; and Notes prints a page per slide with any notes you entered for each slide included below, as shown in Figure 3.25. If you choose Slides, Normal view, or Notes, the only settings you need to worry about are the print range, number of copies, color/grayscale, and whether you want to scale the output to fit the paper (all described earlier).

However, if you specify that you want to print handouts, another option becomes available in the Handouts section. Here, you can specify that you want to print 1, 2, 3, 4, 6, or 9 slides on a page. If you select 1, 2, or 3, the printout provides an area for the audience members to take notes next to each of the slides, as in Figure 3.26; if you choose more than three slides, only the slides print.

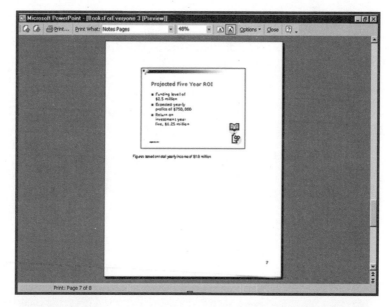

Figure 3.25

Here's the note you added to Slide 7 earlier in the chapter!

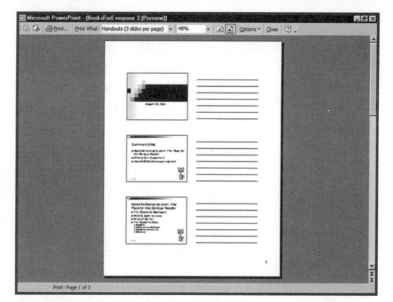

Figure 3.26

This handy area is useful for audience members who want to take notes during your presentation, or make notes after the event.

Once you make all the choices in the Print dialog box, you simply click on OK to print what you've specified. For now, you can close this dialog box by clicking on Cancel and close the current presentation.

ON YOUR OWN

If you want, take a moment to get your own presentation up to speed with the sample by following these steps:

1. Add notes to your presentation. Do this by displaying any slide you want to add a note to in Normal view. Click on the Notes area at the bottom of the screen (the area that says Click to add notes) and enter whatever you like.

2. Work with masters. Select View, Masters, Slide Master to display the pair of masters for the presentation title slide and all other slides. Here you can insert graphics and place them on the slides or add footer text such as slide number or date. Remember that you have to make changes separately on the title slide master and the non-title slide master. You can also use the master feature to make changes to the handouts or notes version of your presentation.

3. Preview or print your presentation. If you'd like to see how your presentation will look, use the new-to-this-version Print Preview feature. To make changes to the output device or print multiple copies, you have to work with the Print dialog box (File, Print).

What's Next?

You've mastered masters and become a font of knowledge about fonts. You make notes on slides and print with the best of 'em. Now it's time to go away and come back to the next session at a later time. Here's a sneak preview of what you'll be learning:

- Learn about including clip art, WordArt, drawings, and other kinds of graphics on your slides to create visual interest.
- See how you can support your ideas with charts, graphs, and tables.
- Add borders, colors, and patterns to objects.
- Explore adding animation and sounds to bring multimedia excitement to your presentations.

Adding Visual Interest

- ✿ Supporting your ideas with charts and tables
- ✿ Working with PowerPoint's drawing tools
- ✿ Adding clip art and text boxes to your slides
- ✿ Using color with graphic objects
- ✿ Adding animation and sound effects

Space is at a premium in a business presentation, making concise bullet points and pithy headlines essential. Using visual elements to get your message across not only adds variety to your presentation, but also saves you valuable slide real estate. Some of these visual elements, such as drawings, clip art, and other graphics, can suggest an idea or concept. Others, such as charts and tables, provide a way to get across a wealth of information at a glance.

Providing Support for Your Ideas with Charts and Tables

Charts and tables perform similar functions: They convey a lot of information (often numerical information) with an economy of space. Charts do this with visual representations of data, and tables organize numbers and text into lists in neat columns and rows.

Adding a Content Element to Your Layout

PowerPoint offers a content placeholder in several of its layouts. Content layouts allow you to work with a variety of non-text objects, including clip art, diagrams, tables, pictures, media events, and charts. Once you have chosen a layout with a Content object, you can click on the appropriate icon to insert one of these objects.

The first step to adding any of these items to a slide is to select a layout that includes a content element. You did that in Session 3 when you chose a layout for Slide 7 that contained a title, bullet list, and content object; Slide 7 is shown in Figure 4.1.

To help you review the process of applying a content layout, you'll start by creating a new Slide 8, using a layout with a content object. A new slide appears after the slide you have displayed.

1. Open the PowerPoint presentation you completed in the last session, or open the file named BooksForEveryone 3 from the CD.

2. Display the Normal view and select Slide 7 in the Outline view.

3. Select Insert, New Slide (or press Ctrl+M). A blank slide appears with the default text layout; the Slide Layout pane appears to its right.

4. Locate the layout called Title & Content. (Remember, its name is displayed when you move your mouse over its preview.)

5. Click on the arrow along the side of the Content layout preview, and select Apply to Selected Slides from the menu that appears.

Figure 4.1

Several slide layouts include content objects.

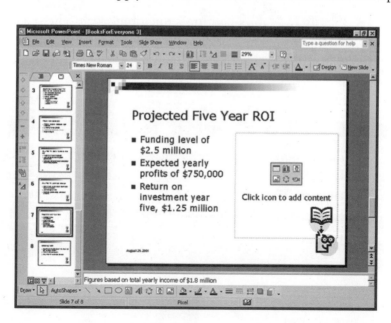

6. Save the presentation to your hard drive with the name Books-ForEveryone 4.

Your new slide now contains a title element and content element, as shown in Figure 4.2.

Working with Tables

Now that you've got a slide with a content object, you can easily create a table. Tables consist of columns and rows that intersect, forming individual cells where you can enter text or numbers. Tables also use gridlines to divide the rows and columns (although you can modify how gridlines are used, as you'll see).

● ●

NOTE PowerPoint uses a "light" version of the table feature in Word; although it offers many of the capabilities of the more robust feature that you'll recognize, it doesn't offer them all.

● ●

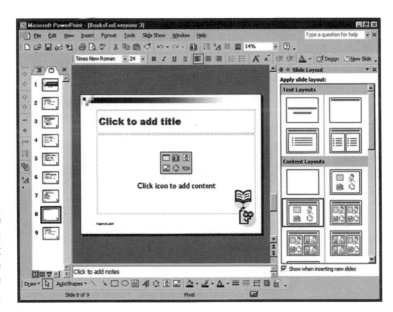

Figure 4.2

Remember that the title and content placeholders are established by the choice of layout.

Creating a Table

The content object in a layout contains icons for six types of graphic objects: a table, chart, clip art, picture, diagram or organization chart, and media clip. To insert one of those objects, you simply click on its icon.

NOTE You can create only one of the six kinds of graphic items in any single content object. If you place one kind of graphic there and then decide you'd like to place a different type of graphic, select the current item (table, graph, or whatever), and press Delete. The placeholder returns to its blank state with all six icons available to you.

Now create a table by following these steps:

1. With the new Slide 8 displayed, click on the table icon on the content object. An Insert Table dialog box like the one shown in Figure 4.3 appears.

2. Use the counter arrows on the Number of columns item to set it to 4 columns.

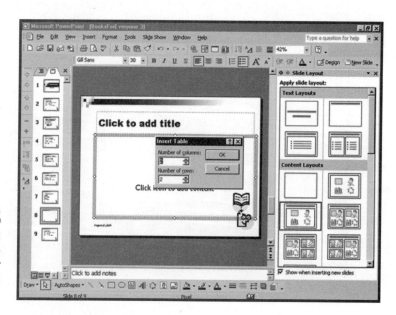

Figure 4.3

This simple dialog box allows you to set the size of your table in rows and columns.

3. Use the counter arrows on the Number of rows item to set it to 4 rows.

4. Click OK to accept the settings. A table with four rows and four columns appears, as shown in Figure 4.4.

◆ ◆

You can create a table of up to 25 rows and columns using these steps, but be forewarned: Using a table with more than five or six rows or columns makes its contents difficult for your audience to read.

◆ ◆

Entering Table Contents

Entering information in a table is simple. You click in any cell in the table and start typing. Longer text automatically wraps down a line. If you want to move from one cell to the cell to its right, you press the Tab key. If you want to move back one cell to the left, you press Shift+Tab.

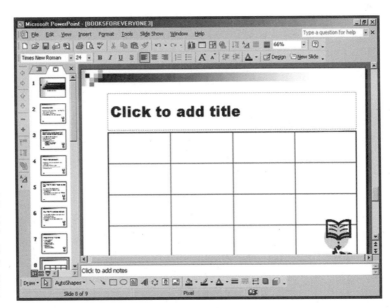

Figure 4.4

Don't worry about the way the master slide graphic overlaps the new table; you'll fix that shortly!

Now it's time to fill in your table. Enter the title and cell contents you see in Figure 4.5 by following these steps:

1. Click in the title object; it opens for editing.

2. Type the title **Books Online: An Industry Overview**.

3. Click in the top-left cell of the table and enter the text shown in the figure (**Company**).

4. Press tab, and enter the information in the next cell.

5. Continue to follow these steps until all the text is entered.

Now that you've entered the contents of the table, it's time to pay a bit of attention to the formatting of the table.

Formatting Tables

You can do several things to format tables in PowerPoint:

✿ Change the formatting of text in a table (font, font size, italic, bold, underline, and so on).

✿ Change the style of the table outside and inside border lines.

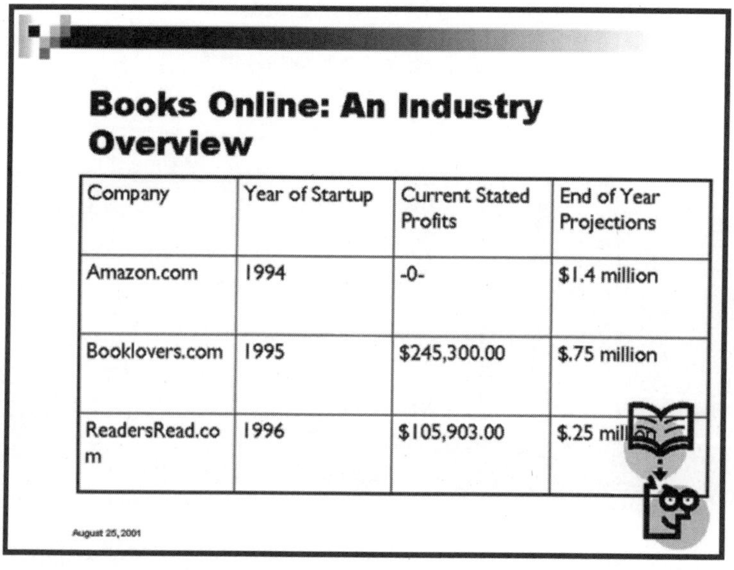

Figure 4.5

Tables provide an organized, at-a-glance way to present information.

Books Online: An Industry Overview

Company	Year of Startup	Current Stated Profits	End of Year Projections
Amazon.com	1994	-0-	$1.4 million
Booklovers.com	1995	$245,300.00	$.75 million
ReadersRead.com	1996	$105,903.00	$.25 million

August 25, 2001

✪ Add color to cells.

✪ Adjust text alignment within cells.

There are two methods of working on table formatting: You can select View, Toolbars, Tables & Borders and display the toolbar shown in Figure 4.6; or you can work in the Format Table dialog box shown in Figure 4.7.

Modifying Borders

Start by working on borders, including the gridlines that define the table cells. For that, I recommend using the Format Table dialog box because of its one-stop list of all border features on a single tab:

1. Click on the outside edge of the table to select it. (Clicking within a cell of the table places your insertion point in the cell ready for entering text.)

2. Select Format, Table.

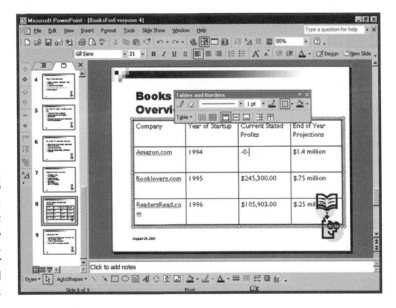

Figure 4.6

Besides formatting features, the toolbar offers tools for editing tables, such as an eraser to erase individual lines between cells.

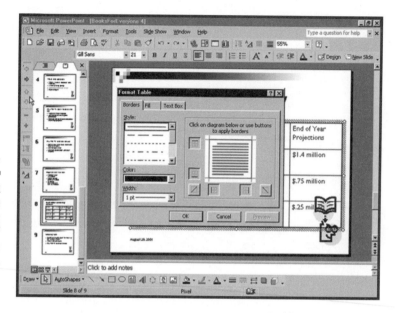

Figure 4.7

The dialog box provides some visual aides, such as a preview of how applying different borders will look in a table cell.

3. Using the diagram of borders in the dialog box shown in Figure 4.7, click on the buttons for the top, bottom, and two side borders to remove them.

4. Click on the Width drop-down list and change the width of the border lines to $1^1/_2$ pt.

5. Click OK to apply the changes.

Your table now sports a minimal look with fewer borderlines. The next step is to take care of a problem with the text in the Company column; the text for the last item in the column breaks in a bad spot. You can deal with that by resizing the column:

1. Move your mouse over the line between the first and second columns until your cursor changes into two lines with arrows pointing to either side.

2. Click and drag the line slightly to the right, until the cells in Column 1 all fit their text on one line, and then release your mouse.

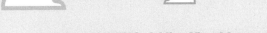

3. Repeat Step 2 to modify the width of the third column so all the numbers fit in one row.

4. Click anywhere outside the table.

Your table should now look like the one in Figure 4.8.

Working with Table Text

Formatting text in tables is pretty much like formatting text anywhere. You can change the font and the font size, add effects such as bold, italic, or underline, and change the color of the text.

NOTE You can find out more about formatting text on PowerPoint slides by peeking back at the Saturday Afternoon chapter.

For now, you'll make the top row headings in your table bold and modify the font to be in line with the rest of your presentation:

Figure 4.8

You can move column and row lines as you like to make text fit efficiently.

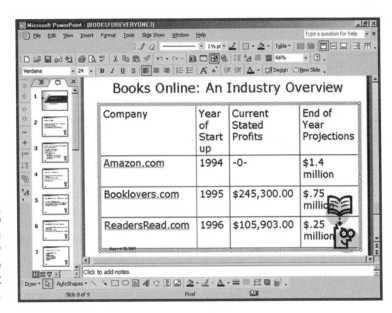

1. Click to the left of the text in the first cell and drag to the right to highlight all the text in the first row.

2. Click the Bold button on the Formatting toolbar.

3. Select Edit, Select All (or press Ctrl+A).

4. Open the Font drop-down menu and scroll down to the font named Verdana.

5. Click on Verdana to apply it to the selected text.

Don't worry about the master slide graphic that's covering up the text in one table cell; you'll fix that later in this session. However, we've introduced an old problem by changing the font: Because letters in different fonts aren't always the same size, our first column text is now larger than before and breaking to a second line at awkward points. You can fix that by modifying the font size:

1. Click to the left of the text Amazon.com and drag to the right and down to highlight the rest of the cells in the table (excluding the column headings).

2. Click on the arrow to the right of the Font Size tool on the Formatting toolbar and select 18 pt from the drop-down list that appears.

Your slide should now look like the one in Figure 4.9.

Adding Color to Tables

You can use color in tables to emphasize or draw attention to certain information or to simply bring the colors in line with the color scheme used in the slide design you've applied to your slides. You can apply color to several elements in tables. You can change the color of the border lines (using the color drop-down list on the Borders tab of the Format Table dialog box) and the text (by selecting it and using the Text Color tool on the Formatting toolbar) or add a fill color to cells, which you'll do now. In this table, you can use a color fill to highlight the end-of-year projections of companies in the table to draw the audience's attention to them:

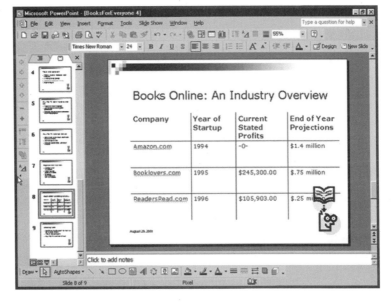

Figure 4.9

You can make text
fit comfortably in
each cell in several
ways, including
changing font size,
widening columns,
or inserting manual
breaks.

1. Click to the left of the text in the second cell of the fourth column,
   $1.4 million, and drag down to highlight it and the two cells
   beneath it.

2. Select Format, Table. The Format Table dialog box appears.

3. Select the Fill tab to display it (see Figure 4.10).

4. Click the arrow on the drop-down color menu and select a color,
   such as a red or green, by clicking on it.

5. Check the Semitransparent checkbox. This choice softens the color
   and makes text in the colored cells easier to read.

Figure 4.10

Make your table
more colorful using
settings in this
dialog box.

6. Click OK to apply the fill color.

7. Click anywhere outside of the table.

8. Save the file.

Now your slide offers a focal point for the audience's attention; if they read nothing else on this table, they will notice the end-of-year profit projections.

Working with Charts

The Chart feature of PowerPoint is helpful whenever you need to represent numerical data visually. Charts come in a variety of styles, from simple bar charts to pie charts, charts with multiple columns, and 3-D surface charts.

The chart feature of PowerPoint is a shared feature for all Office programs, so you may have seen it before. With it, you can do some pretty fancy things. You can modify gridlines and text labels for elements, add 3-D effects, format chart text and colors, and add a legend as a guide to chart elements, for example. For now, you'll add a bar chart to this slide and make some formatting adjustments.

Inserting a Bar Chart in Your Presentation

When you first insert a chart, PowerPoint opens the chart program and places a multiple-column bar chart on your slide and opens a datasheet for editing, as shown in Figure 4.11. A datasheet is a simple spreadsheet. The information in the first column specifies the types of data contained in each of the bars; the information in the first row represents the data along the bottom or y-axis of the chart, although you can change the chart/data orientation if you like. The data you enter in the cells that are formed by the intersection of that column and row provide the numerical values represented by the bars themselves.

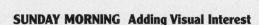

ON YOUR OWN

In addition to standard charts that work well for reporting numerical data, PowerPoint allows you to create diagrams and organizational charts. If you want a chart showing an organizational structure or workflow, use the Insert Diagram or Organization Chart icon in any layout containing a content object. This is a new feature in PowerPoint 2002, and offers much more sophisticated options than the old Organization Chart feature.

Using this feature you can choose a style for your organization chart; add nodes to the chart; designate how objects on the chart that represent subordinates, co-workers, and assistants should branch; add text to the nodes of the chart. In addition, you can modify connecting lines, and even display or hide various levels of detail.

Features for working with diagrams include choices of style, the ability to add text captions to the elements of the diagram, and the ability to scale the diagram to different sizes. You can edit text in objects by clicking on them.

On this slide, you will show the projected income and profits for this company over the first five years of its existence. Note that as income rises over this time period, profit is projected to stay steady because of increasing investments in building the company, such as adding employees and additional visitor support costs. Create the data for your chart with these steps:

1. Click in the heading of the second column, which opens it for editing.

2. Type **1st Yr**.

3. Press Tab to move to the next cell to the right.

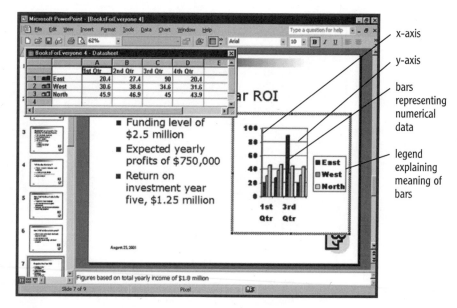

Figure 4.11

The datasheet is the source of information shown on your chart.

4. Type **2nd Yr**.

5. Continue pressing Tab or clicking in cells and entering new text as shown in the following table.

6. Click anywhere outside of the chart to close the datasheet and return to the slide, which now looks like the slide shown in Figure 4.12.

7. Save the file.

TABLE 4.1					
	1st Yr	2nd Yr	3rd Yr	4th Yr	5th Yr
Income	1,000	1,000	1,250	1,750	2,000
Profits	750	750	750	750	750

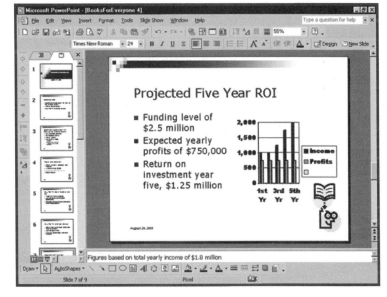

Figure 4.12

The dual bars for each year show projected financial trends for the company.

You'll notice some problems with how information is fitting on this chart: In the legend, a word breaks in the middle, for example. You can take care of that with some formatting tricks.

Formatting a Chart

When you enter data into the datasheet of a chart, small details quite often need attention. This chart has issues with the legend: One word breaks oddly. You can easily fix that by modifying the font being used for the chart:

1. Double-click on any text on the chart.

2. The Format Chart Area dialog box appears, as shown in Figure 4.13.

3. Using the scrollbar on the font list, scroll down to the font Verdana and click on it to select it.

4. In the Font Style list, click on Regular to remove the bold effect from the text.

5. Click OK to apply the formatting and close the dialog box.

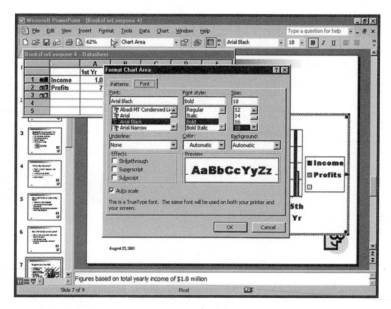

Figure 4.13

This might look familiar because it has most of the same settings as PowerPoint's standard Font dialog box.

Things look better now, with the words in the legend on a single line and the labels a bit easier to read without the bold font. However, there's one more problem: the third item on the legend. By default, the bar chart includes lines for three sets of data, but you only need two. You have to delete the third line so it doesn't show up on the legend:

1. Click on the gray box to the left of the fourth line down on the datasheet (the one labeled 3) to select it.

2. Press Delete.

3. Click anywhere outside of the graph to return to PowerPoint.

4. Save the file.

The chart now looks like the one shown in Figure 4.14, with a correct legend and easy-to-read bars. Notice that depending on the size of a chart it might display every other label (in this case years) rather than every one because of the available space. You can adjust text size to modify this.

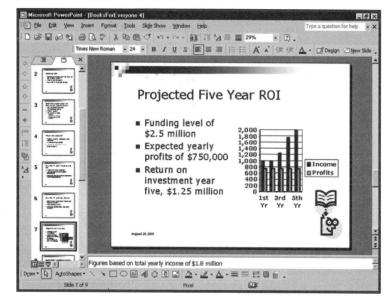

Figure 4.14

A bar chart is perfect for showing trends or comparing two or more data sets.

CHART YOUR OPTIONS

Many more things about a chart can be formatted or modified, including axes, data labels, legends, titles, the walls of 3-D charts, and gridlines. By modifying these elements you can make your chart more readable and offer different perspectives on your data.

You can also use literally dozens of chart types including area charts, pie charts, and radar charts. Each chart type offers choices of variations on that type such as 3-D versions, chart elements that stack on top of each other or display from left to right, and various contour effects. You can also control the display of different styles of charts, for example by modifying the angle of 3-D charts. Although you don't have time to see them all this weekend, explore the feature to see what it has to offer when you need to represent numerical data in a visual way.

ON YOUR OWN

Time to catch up with your own presentation, if you like. Follow these steps to insert a chart or table on a slide:

1.   Insert a new slide.

2.   Change the layout to one with a content placeholder on it.

3.   Click on either the table or chart icon in the placeholder.

4.   If you are entering a table, designate how many rows and columns it will have.

5.   Enter your information in the table or the chart datasheet.

6.   Double-click on various objects on a chart and apply any formatting to gridlines, axis, text, or labels using the dia log box that appears.

Taking a Break

Although you haven't been working all that long, I'll tell you a secret: You've got a pretty long session coming up working with graphics and animation. This is fun stuff, so I don't think you'll be bored, but it might be a good idea to get up and take a stretch before you dive in.

Working with Graphic Elements

Pictures can be worth a thousand words; they can also add visual interest, reinforce a message, and help establish company or product branding.

PowerPoint allows you to place a graphic file on a slide if it is saved in most of the common graphics file formats. A graphic can be a photograph, a simple line drawing, or an elaborate illustration created in a design program. You can use Office's built-in gallery of illustrations and photos called clip art or a graphics file you might have access to.

TIP You can also use features in PowerPoint to pull images directly from a scanner or digital camera. You have to connect those devices to your computer and then use the Insert, Picture, From Scanner or Camera command.

Adding Clip Art to Your Presentation

You might remember placing clip art on the master slide in the last session; however, you didn't place any art on the title slide master. It's time to go through the process in slow motion with that slide so you can learn the details of using clip art.

PowerPoint's clip art feature actually includes access to illustrations, photographs, animations, and sound clips. A valuable catalog feature also allows you to add graphic and multimedia files of your own and set them up to be searchable by keywords.

Finding the Right Clip Art

Inserting a piece of clip art on a slide is easy: It's a matter of a single click. What you need to learn about it is how to navigate the clip art catalog to find the right item for your presentation.

Clip art searches use three criteria.

✿ First, the files are stored in collections; you can search the My Collections folder where you store your own graphic and multimedia files for use in presentations or search previously stored clips in the Office or Web collection.

⚙ Clip art also uses keywords to allow you to search for files. Each media file can have several keywords associated with it.

⚙ Finally, you can control your search by designating the types of media files you want found, such as video or sound.

Using these search criteria, you could, for example, indicate that you want to search only Web collections for any photograph with which the keyword *animals* is associated.

You start by opening the Insert Clip Art pane, which you do by following these steps:

1. In Normal view, use the scrollbar to the right of the slide list to display the title slide of the presentation.

2. Select Insert, Picture, Clip Art from the menu shown in Figure 4.15.

TIP You can also change the slide layout to include a content object and then click on the Clip Art icon within that object to display the Insert Clip Art pane.

3. In the Insert Clip Art pane that appears, click on the Results should be drop-down list to open it, as shown in Figure 4.16.

Figure 4.15

Through this menu, you can insert directly from a file on your computer or network, or from a scanner or camera, as well as through clip art collections.

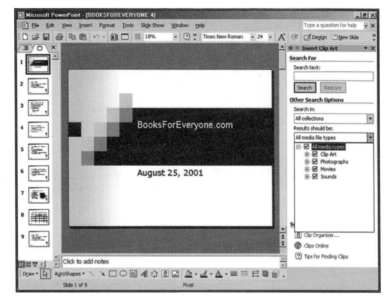

Figure 4.16

If only movies, sounds, or photos, will do for your presentation, you can narrow your search by media type.

4. Click on the Movies and Sounds checkboxes to deselect them; for our purposes, photos and clip art illustrations are all we need.

5. Enter the word **books** in the Search Text text box.

6. Click on Search. The previews shown in Figure 4.17 appear.

Now, all you need to do is make a choice!

Inserting Clip Art

Scroll down through the preview items using the scrollbar to the right of them to see the wide variety of graphics files PowerPoint associates with the keyword "books."

TIP

It's usually a good idea to place graphics of a similar style in a presentation. That could mean that you use all black and white line drawings or all color illustrations with a cartoon-like feeling, for example. This practice helps give your presentation a sense of unity.

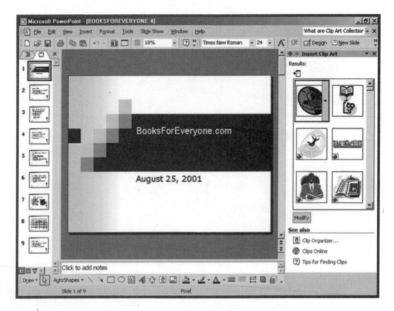

Figure 4.17

Every file that matches your criteria is displayed as a preview here.

Locate the picture shown in Figure 4.18, or one similar to it, and click on the preview to insert it on your slide. The image appears in the middle of your slide, as shown in Figure 4.18.

Figure 4.18

The graphic object is displayed on your slide, along with a Picture toolbar to modify it.

NOTE You can also insert any graphic file you might have available without going through the clip art feature. Simply select Insert, Picture, From File and then browse to locate the file name using the dialog box that appears. The image contained in that file is placed on your slide. You can move and resize the object..

Moving and Resizing Clip Art

When you insert a clip art object on a slide, it is selected for editing, with the Picture toolbar displayed. This toolbar contains tools that allow you to modify the brightness, contrast, and color of a graphic object.

For now, you'll work with moving the clip art object you just inserted on the title slide so that it doesn't overlap the title of the slide. Then, you'll resize the clip art object on the master slide because it interferes with other slide contents, as in Slides 7 and 8 that contain a table and chart:

1. Move your mouse over the object until the cursor turns into a four-way arrow.

2. Click and drag the object to the bottom-right corner, as shown in Figure 4.19.

3. Select View, Master, Slide Master, and click on the Slide Master preview to display it (rather than the Title Master).

4. Click in the round handle on the top-left corner of the clip art object and drag down and to the right to make it smaller.

5. You'll see a small dotted outline of the image as you drag, indicating the resized image, as shown in Figure 4.20. Release your mouse when the dotted outline indicates the image is about a third smaller than it was originally, as in Figure 4.20.

6. Click on the Close Master View button on the Slide Master View toolbar. This piece of art should now co-exist with any other objects on all slides without overlapping them.

7. Save the presentation.

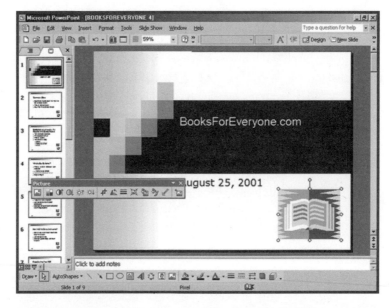

Figure 4.19

It's easy to move clip art around a slide with the click-and-drag method.

Figure 4.20

The dotted line shows the size this object will be if you release your mouse at this point.

◆◆◆◆◆◆◆◆◆◆◆◆◆◆◆◆◆◆◆◆◆◆◆◆◆◆◆◆◆◆◆◆

CAUTION Resizing by clicking on any of the corner handles maintains the proportions of the original image. Resizing by dragging on any of the other handles on the top, bottom, or sides distorts the image from its original proportions.

◆◆◆◆◆◆◆◆◆◆◆◆◆◆◆◆◆◆◆◆◆◆◆◆◆◆◆◆◆◆◆◆

Using PowerPoint's Drawing Tools

You don't have to use somebody else's art in your presentation: You can draw your own using PowerPoint's Drawing feature. You can draw diagrams, add starbursts and text boxes, and create drawings of lines, circles, and other shapes. You can group drawings into a single object, add color, and apply other types of formatting to them.

Creating Drawings

You create drawings in PowerPoint using the Drawing toolbar, which is shown in Figure 4.21 with one of its menus, AutoShapes, displayed. This toolbar also contains tools for formatting drawing objects.

Figure 4.21

The AutoShapes pop-up menu offers dozens of preconfigured drawing choices.

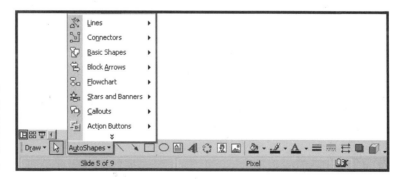

You're going to build a drawing of a truck on Slide 5, titled "How Will We Drive Traffic to Our Site?" So the slide is not too busy, you'll also omit the graphic object placed there by the master slide feature.

Follow these steps to omit the master graphic and draw the body of the truck using the rectangle tool:

1. Display Slide 5 in Normal view.

2. Right-click on the slide and select Background from the shortcut menu that appears. The Background dialog box shown in Figure 4.22 appears.

3. Click in the checkbox for Omit background graphics from master to turn on that option.

4. Click on Apply. (Don't click on Apply to All, or the graphic will disappear from your presentation entirely!) The graphic placed by the slide master disappears from this slide; notice that the slide design graphics have also disappeared because they are part of the master slide.

Figure 4.22

You can use this dialog box to specify background colors on your slides.

TIP

> Because it can undermine the continuity of your presentation design to remove the background design from a single slide in order to get rid of a master graphic, you should consider the option of applying a different slide master to that slide—one that uses the same background but not the graphic. However, omitting the master graphics is a quick solution you may sometimes need to use.

5. Select View, Toolbar, Drawing to display the Drawing toolbar.

6. Click on the Rectangle button on the Drawing toolbar.

7. Place your mouse cursor, which has become a crosshatch, near the bottom third of the slide and click and drag to draw a rectangle like the one shown in Figure 4.23. When the rectangle is about the right size, release your mouse button.

8. Click on the Rectangle tool again, and this time, draw the front of the truck; a smaller rectangle placed right in front of the first one, as shown in Figure 4.24.

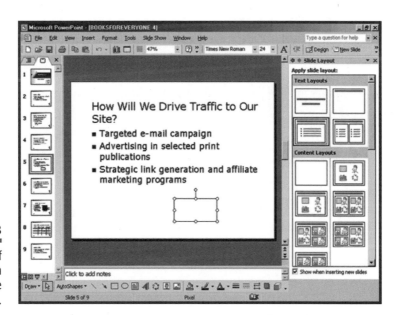

Figure 4.23

Here's the body of your truck drawn with a single motion.

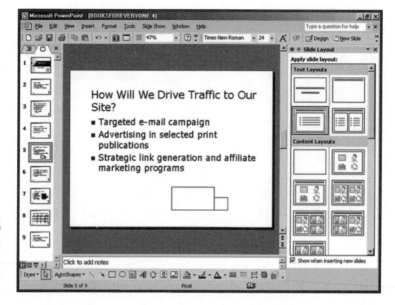

Figure 4.24

You can build drawings using several shapes in combination.

Your drawing objects might appear with a fill color or with no fill color (as these figures show) depending on the last choices made in PowerPoint's drawing feature. If your objects appear with a fill color, that's okay: You'll work with fill color shortly to see how to modify those settings.

You can use any of the other drawing tools such as Oval and Line to draw shapes in the same way. But I'm about to let you in on a shortcut for drawing more complex shapes: PowerPoint's AutoShapes.

Using AutoShapes

AutoShapes are simple drawing-object tools that allow you to draw shapes such as stars or banners with the same click-and-drag method you used to draw a rectangle. They can be a real time-saver in creating drawings for your presentation. You'll use AutoShapes now to add tires to your truck:

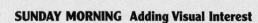

1. Click on the AutoShapes menu to open it.

2. Select Flowchart; a side menu opens, as you can see in Figure 4.25.

3. Click on the shape in the fifth row down on the left of this menu—a circle with a diagonal crosshatch in it.

4. Click on the slide just under the back of the truck and drag to draw a small tire with this tool.

TIP While using drawing tools, you can constrain rounded objects to stay in a circle shape, rather than an ellipse shape, by holding down the Shift key as you draw the object.

5. Release your mouse button when the tire is big enough; it should just touch the bottom of the truck.

6. Right-click on the tire object and select Copy from the shortcut menu that appears.

7. Click the Paste button on the Standard toolbar, or press Ctrl+V to place the copy of the AutoShape you drew on your slide.

8. Move your mouse over the copy until the cursor becomes a four-way arrow; drag the copy of the tire to place it under the front of the truck and release your mouse button.

Figure 4.25

All of the items here offer additional menus of choices, except the More AutoShapes choice, which displays more shapes in the Clip Art pane.

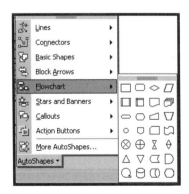

9. Click anywhere outside of the drawing to see how it looks and save your file. Your drawing should now look like the one in Figure 4.26.

TIP Why did I have you copy the AutoShape rather than insert a second one? Because you determine the proportions of an AutoShape as you draw it, it's not always easy to draw exactly the same size object with the same length and width. For that reason, if you're creating two objects that should be identical, it's often wiser to insert the first object and then make a copy of it.

Grouping Objects on a Slide

Now that you've created a drawing made up of several smaller objects, it's a good idea to group those objects. Right now, the rectangles and AutoShapes that make up your truck are separate; if you want to move your truck on the page, you have to move each item separately. Grouping

Figure 4.26

Now your drawing is starting to look like a semi-truck with very little effort on your part.

allows you to stick the smaller objects together to become one object. You can then move that object with one move, apply formatting to all of its elements at once, and resize it as one object.

Follow these steps to group your drawing objects:

1. Click on one object to select it.

2. Click on the slide and drag to include all the objects on the slide until a box appears surrounding them; they are now all selected, as shown in Figure 4.27.

3. Select Draw, Group from the Drawing toolbar.

4. Save the file.

The items are now grouped, with a single set of resizing handles.

Applying Colors and Modifying Line Styles

It's time to have some fun with your little work of art. Adding color to objects can add interest or realism to a line drawing, and it's so easy to do.

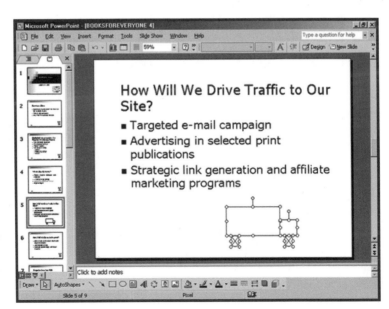

Figure 4.27

Resizing handles on all the objects indicate they are selected.

Follow these steps to add color to an object:

1. Click on the object to select it.

2. Click on the Fill Color button on the Drawing toolbar. If your object already has a fill color and you want to get rid of it, this is where you choose No Fill. If you want to fill it with color, this is where you can select a color to do that. A handful of the most recently chosen colors appear in this menu, but you can choose from a much broader range.

3. Click on the More Fill Colors item on this menu to see the Colors dialog box shown in Figure 4.28.

4. Click on a dark green color in the color area; a preview of it appears in the New/Current preview in the bottom-right corner of this dialog box.

5. Click OK to apply the fill color.

Your object is filled with a solid green color.

Figure 4.28

A rainbow of colors is available to you from this dialog box.

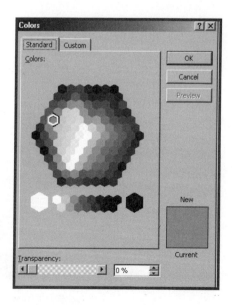

TIP You can also use the Fill Color menu to add various effects to your drawings. If you click on the Fill Color button on the Drawing toolbar and then on Fill Effects, you get a four-tab dialog box where you can set patterns, textures, and a gradient effect or even place a photograph inside your object.

NOTE If several objects on a slide contain color and you want them to overlap, you can use a feature on the Draw menu on the Drawing toolbar that lets you set the order of those objects. Using the Order feature, you can bring a selected object to the front of the grouping so its shape and color hide other objects in the grouping or send it to the back so it's hidden by overlapping objects.

Adding Text to a Drawing

Although you've been adding text to slides using PowerPoint layout place-holders up to now, you can add text objects using the Drawing toolbar. However, you should be aware that when you add text this way, it does not appear in the slide show outline (which in this case is fine!).

NOTE The Drawing toolbar actually has two tools for placing text on a slide. In addition to the Text Box tool, you can use the WordArt item to add text. The WordArt application lets you insert text with special effects applied, such as curved text or text that runs down a page vertically. WordArt can be fun, and it is simple to use, but take care: These elaborate text effects can be hard for an audience to read on a slide.

Time to add one final touch to your drawing object before you move on: You'll add the name of the Web site, BooksForEveryone.com, to the side of the truck. You can do this in two ways: Click on a drawing object and simply type text, which will appear centered in the object; or draw a text box on the object. Drawing a text box has the benefit of allowing you to move the text object around within the drawing object.

Follow these steps to add a text box to the truck drawing:

1. Click on the Text Box button on the Drawing toolbar.

2. Click in the middle of the truck.

3. Type **BooksforEveryone.com**. Don't worry that it's too big to fit in the drawing; you'll modify the text formatting now.

4. Click and drag to select the text you just entered.

5. Select Format, Font.

6. In the Font dialog box that appears, make these changes: Choose Arial as the font, make it bold, change the color to yellow, and set the font size at 12 pt.

7. Click OK to apply the changes.

You might have to click on the text box and move it around slightly to fit it on the truck body or make the font size slightly smaller if your truck is smaller than the one I drew. When you've finished, your drawing should look like the one in Figure 4.29.

NOTE There's no reason to change the orientation of this truck on your slide, but if you'd drawn an airplane instead, you might want to show it at an angle, as if it's taking off. To do that, you just grab a selected object by the green handle above it, and twist it around to rotate it to any angle you like.

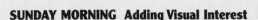

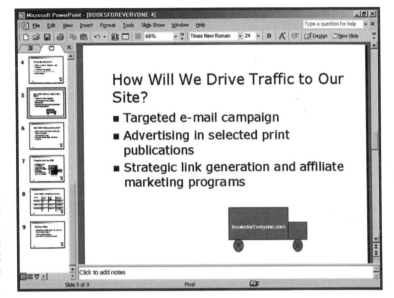

Figure 4.29

Combining drawings with text can help you get your message across.

Working with Multimedia

Illustrations and photographs on a slide can add visual interest, but if you really want to make your audience sit up and take notice, try using some multimedia in your presentation. Multimedia options include animated sequences and sound effects that you play back during your presentation.

Adding Animation

Animation in PowerPoint can refer to animated clips that show a figure running or a building tumbling down, for example. Animation can also add movement to text and objects you've placed on your slide. Another use for animation schemes is to insert transition effects as you move from one slide to another during a presentation. (You'll work with animation schemes, a feature new to PowerPoint 2002, in the next session when you set up your slide show.)

Animation should not be overdone, but if used sparingly, it can make a clever comment on a slide topic, add a bit of humor, or offer a bit of relief from the many words on your slides.

In this section, you'll add an animation clip to a slide and animate text on another.

Inserting a Media Clip on a Slide

You add animation to a slide by using the Clip Art pane and insert a movie file rather than an illustration. You have a few options for how you do this:

- ✿ You can change your slide layout to contain a content object and then click on the Insert Media Clip icon.
- ✿ Alternately, you can use the Insert menu to insert a movie or sound.

Either of these steps opens the Clip Art pane with movies displayed, as shown in Figure 4.30, and places a content object on your slide.

Use one of these options now to place a media clip on a slide:

1. Display Slide 4, titled "Who Is Our Customer?"
2. Select Insert, Movies and Sounds, Movies from Clip Organizer. The Insert Clip Art pane appears, with animation clips displayed.
3. Scroll down until you locate an animation with a person or people in it.
4. If you'd like to preview the animation, click on the arrow along its right side to display a menu and select Preview/Properties. The dialog box shown in Figure 4.31 appears.
5. The animation plays repeatedly. When you're done previewing it, click Close to close the dialog box.
6. When you find an animation you like, click on it to insert it on your slide, which should now contain the preview image, as shown in Figure 4.32.

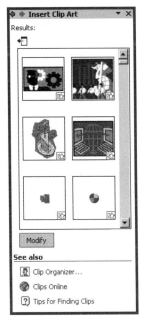

Figure 4.30

Each of these previews represents an animated sequence.

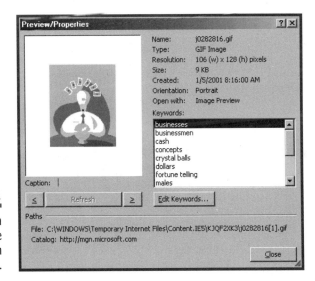

Figure 4.31

Learn all about an animation before you place it on your slide.

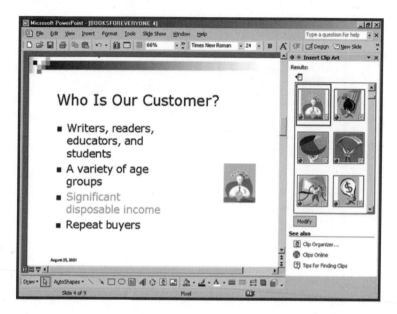

Figure 4.32

The animation sits still…until you run your slide show.

Take a peek at how your animation will appear in your actual slide show:

1. Click on the Slide Show view icon at the bottom-left corner of PowerPoint's window.

2. When you're done enjoying the animation, press Escape to leave Slide Show.

3. Save the presentation.

Working with Custom Animations

You might find that you want to add animation to things you place on your slides yourself, such as text or pictures. You do that in PowerPoint with custom animations.

The Custom Animation feature allows you to add animation effects to selected objects, designate what action starts the animation (such as clicking your mouse) and the speed of the animation.

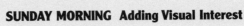

Animating Text and Objects

What if the truck you just drew could drive across your slide when it appears in your presentation? That would not only catch people's eye, but also reinforce the slide's topic of driving traffic to your site.

Follow these steps to get your truck in motion:

1. Display Slide 5, on which you drew a truck earlier.
2. Right-click on the object, and select Custom Animation from the shortcut menu that appears. The Custom Animation pane appears to the right of your screen.
3. Click on the Add Effect button; a menu is displayed.
4. Select Motion Paths, Draw Custom Path, Curve. This provides you with a tool to draw a route for your truck across the slide.
5. Click on the far left of the slide and move your mouse a small distance to the right; a line appears as you do.
6. Click to anchor that portion of the curve and then drag down to another point on the slide, heading down toward the truck's final position, as shown in Figure 4.33.
7. Continue to drag and click to create a curved path for your truck.
8. When you've reached the middle of the truck object, double-click to turn off the Curve tool. The animation now previews automatically.
9. Save the presentation.

If you want to see how the animation looks in a slide show, click on the Slide Show button in the bottom of the Custom Animation pane. Press Escape when you're done to return to Normal view.

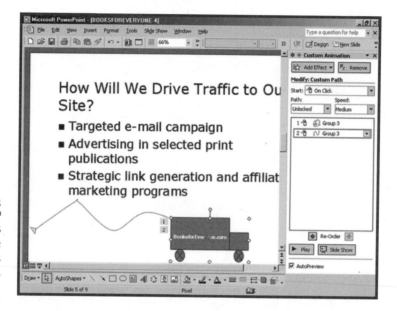

Figure 4.33

This curvy path is
the road your little
truck will travel as
your slide is
displayed.

TIP To show animations in a presentation you publish on the Web, select File, Save As Web Page. From the dialog box that appears, click on Publish and then on Web Options. On the General tab of the dialog box that follows, select Show Slide Animations While Browsing and then continue to publish the presentation to the Web. Learn more about this process in Sunday afternoon's session.

Adding Sound Effects

When you were watching your animated truck driving across the slide, I bet you said to yourself, wouldn't it be great if I could add a little whooshing sound to reinforce the sense of motion of the truck? Of course it would, and it's easy to do. You must select the animation and display the Custom Animation pane. (You can right-click the object and choose Custom Animation from the shortcut menu, if you've closed the pane since the last section.) Then, follow these steps to add a sound:

1. When you created an animation, a new group item appeared (called Group 3 in Figure 4.34) in a list in the middle of the Custom Animation pane. Click the arrow on the right of the item to display the menu shown in Figure 4.34.

2. Select the command Effect Options from the menu. The Custom Path dialog box shown in Figure 4.35 appears.

3. Click on the Sound drop-down list and select the Whoosh sound.

4. Click on the Timing tab.

5. In the Start drop-down list, select With Previous. This choice plays the sound as the previous slide disappears and this one appears.

6. Click OK to save the settings and see a preview of the entire animation, including the sound.

The Custom Path dialog box also allows you to set an effect on an animated object that dims or changes its color after it has played and to set timing to occur when you click your mouse, rather than automatically as slides change. You might choose, for example, to include

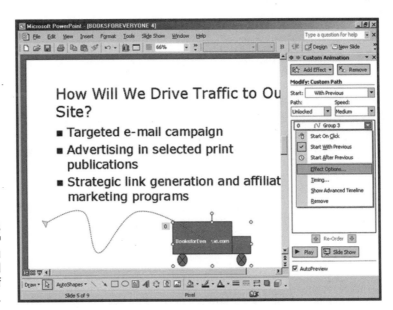

Figure 4.34

This menu lets you control timing and other features of the animation.

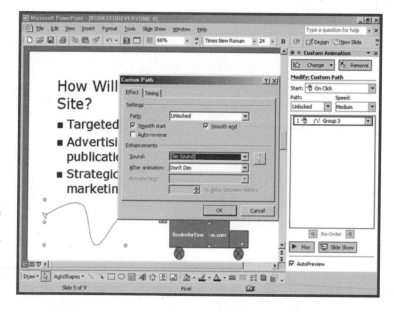

Figure 4.35

Control timing and sound effects for your animated drawing from this dialog box.

an animation of coins that "jingle" when you click on a text object that includes the word "Profits". The Timing tab also has settings that control the speed of animation playback and allow you to repeat the animation as many times as you like.

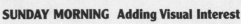
ON YOUR OWN

Time to get your own presentation up to speed with the things we've done in the second half of this session. Perform these actions to add visual appeal to your slides:

- Either apply a layout with a content object, or select Insert, Picture, Clip Art to display the Insert Clip Art pane. From here, you can search for illustrations or photos and click on a preview to insert it on a slide.

- Draw your own visual elements using the Drawing toolbar. Display it by selecting View, Toolbars, Drawing. Click on drawing tools such as the Rectangle or Oval to draw objects, or use the AutoShapes menu to access more sophisticated drawing tools.

- You can move, resize, group, change line style, or add color to drawing objects on a slide.

- You can use a content object on a layout or select Insert, Movies and Sounds to display the Insert Clip Art pane with animation elements.

- You can also use the Custom Animation pane to add animation to text or graphics on a slide and use the Custom Animation dialog box to set sounds and timing for animations.

What's Next?

You are definitely in the home stretch! After playing around with all kinds of clip art and multimedia, this afternoon you'll wrap up by handling any remaining problems in your presentation, setting up your presentation, and navigating through it. Here's what you'll be covering in the next—and last—session:

- Check spelling and proofread for any text or visual errors.
- Apply transitions that occur as your presentation displays a new slide.
- Record a narration for a standalone presentation.
- Learn how to navigate through a slide show.
- Publish your presentation to the Web.

See you this afternoon!

Preparing to Make Your Presentation

- ⚙ Check your spelling
- ⚙ Apply transitions and narration
- ⚙ Practice running your slide show
- ⚙ Learn to use presenter tools
- ⚙ Take your presentation on the road
- ⚙ Publish your presentation on the Web

Take a look back for a moment: Over the past few days, you've created a presentation, added design and layout elements, formatted text, added graphic and multimedia elements, and organized your presentation content. That's a lot to have accomplished, but you have a few more things to do to realize the destiny of any presentation: to be presented.

In this final session, you'll review your presentation for any mistakes or design issues, make settings for presenting your slides, and learn how to actually run your presentation, in person or on the Web. So let's get going!

Giving Your Presentation a Final Check

As with any written document, problems with spelling, grammar, omitted words, and so on can be a PowerPoint presentation's downfall. No matter how brilliant your ideas, if you botch the details, the only thing people might remember is that misspelled word or awkwardly placed graphic on the third slide. You should always proof your presentations for spelling and design problems before finalizing them.

Checking Your Presentation's Spelling

Spelling is a feature of PowerPoint that runs through the words in your presentation, flagging possible misspellings and suggesting correct spellings. It's important that you keep in mind that spelling isn't always straightforward: IBM might be a fine name for a company, but if it isn't in your Spelling dictionary, it is flagged as an incorrectly spelled word. Likewise, if you enter the word fair and what you really meant was fare, no spelling checker in the world can figure that out. Proper names are another item that spelling checkers often call out as errors when they aren't.

To deal with the limitations of spelling checkers, they typically allow you some level of control over what changes they make. The Spelling feature in PowerPoint allows you to do the following:

- Add to PowerPoint's dictionary. If you add a word, it is forevermore considered a correct spelling of a word in all your presentations. Use this for your own last name, your company name, and your product names, for example.

- Ignore a particular instance of a supposed misspelling; this is useful if, for example, an acronym or proper name occurs only once in your document.

- Ignore All causes Spelling to stop checking instances of a word in the document but doesn't actually add the word to your dictionary. This is handy if you use a company name such as Kopy Shop throughout a particular document. You don't want to add Kopy to your dictionary forever because you want to be flagged if you type a k by mistake when entering the word copy.

- AutoCorrect is a feature of PowerPoint that automatically corrects common errors as you type, such as teh for the. AutoCorrect also makes the entry of certain symbols easier; for example, if you type (c), PowerPoint changes it to ©. When performing a spelling

check, you can click on the AutoCorrect button to add a particular term to the AutoCorrect feature to correct it automatically in the future.

✪ Change changes the word to the suggested spelling in the highlighted instance only.

✪ Change All changes the word to the suggested spelling everywhere it appears throughout the document.

Time to check the spelling for this presentation:

1. Open the file named BooksForEveryone4.

2. Display the title slide in Normal view.

3. Select Tools, Spelling. The Spelling dialog box shown in Figure 5.1 appears, with the first word it suspects is misspelled, Books-ForEveryone.com, flagged.

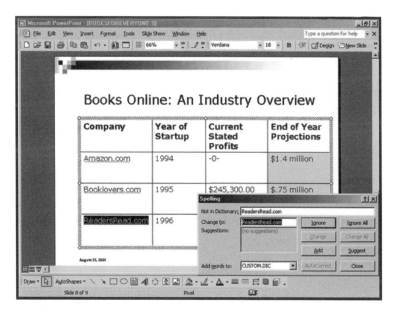

Figure 5.1

Based on its internal dictionary, PowerPoint assumes BooksForEveryone. com is a spelling error.

4. Because this term is correct, and because it's a company name you'll be using all the time, you should add it to your dictionary. Click on Add.

5. Spelling now targets the word booklights, which it correctly suggests should be two words. Click Change to correct the spelling.

6. The word bookcovers is highlighted next for the same reason: PowerPoint says it should be two words. Click Change to correct it.

7. Next, Spelling indicates that the word ReadersRead.com is possibly incorrect, because it can't find a match in its dictionary. Because ReadersRead.com is the name of a Web site and correct (and because it occurs only once in the presentation), click on Ignore.

8. The spelling check goes to the next problematic word: Booklovers.com; although booklovers is one word and therefore spelled correctly, PowerPoint doesn't recognize the .com extension. Again, click Ignore.

9. The spelling checker now highlights Amazon.com: Once again although the spelling of Amazon is correct, the .com is confusing PowerPoint. Click Ignore one more time.

10. A final dialog box appears telling you the spelling check is complete. Click OK to close it.

11. Save the presentation with the name BooksForEveryone5.

Looking for Design Problems

Almost every presentation, no matter how carefully crafted, needs a little finessing before it goes in front of an audience. It's always a good idea to review your slides for design issues, such as:

✿ Graphic objects that overlap text

✿ Titles that break in awkward places

✿ Slides that are crowded with too many bullet lines

✿ Inconsistent use of graphics

✿ Inconsistent use of color

So take a moment to eyeball your presentation. Slide Sorter view is a good place to get a look at all your slides at once. I spot four items that could be cleaned up:

✿ You used a different piece of clip art on the title slide and the slide master; it would be better to make these graphics consistent.

✿ You generated a summary slide early in the process of building slides and have added content since then; you have to update it.

✿ The title on Slide 5, How Will We Drive Traffic to Our Site?, breaks awkwardly.

✿ The placement of the animation graphic on Slide 4 is too close to the master slide graphic and makes the slide look busy; it would be better if we moved it to the top of the slide.

 TIP PowerPoint also includes a feature to check for overall design issues, located on the Spelling and Style tab of the Options dialog box (Tools, Options). It has limited usefulness; you're better off closely eyeballing your presentation contents. The types of problems it checks include the number of fonts allowed to be used in a presentation, length of headings, and number of bullets.

Time to take care of all of these issues; it's a bit of a lengthy exercise, but it makes a good review of the tools and skills you've used throughout the weekend. First, you'll make the clip art image on the Slide Master consistent with the title slide:

1. Select View, Master, Slide Master. The slide master shown in Figure 5.2 appears.

Figure 5.2

This is where that little graphic on most slides is coming from.

2. Right-click on the graphic and select Cut from the shortcut menu that appears.

3. Select Insert, Picture, Clip Art. The Clip Art pane appears.

4. Make sure the Result Should Be field is set to search just Clip Art; if it isn't, deselect any other choices from the drop-down list.

5. Type the Search text books, and click Search.

6. When the results of the search appear, scroll down to locate the graphic you placed on the title slide and click on it to insert it on the slide master, which should then look like Figure 5.3.

7. Place your mouse over the clip art object, click and drag it down to the bottom-right corner of the slide.

8. Click on the left corner handle of the graphic and drag down and to the right to make it about one quarter of its original size.

9. Click on Close Master View to return to your presentation, with the new, consistent graphic in place.

Next, you can deal with the arrangement of the animation icon on Slide 4.

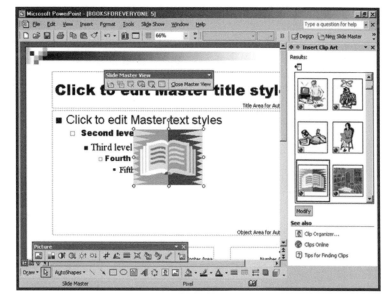

Figure 5.3

Continuity of graphic images help a presentation look more polished and consistent.

10. Display Slide 4 in Normal view

11. Click and drag the Animation graphic to appear to the left of the slide title.

12. Move the slide title to the right so it doesn't overlap the graphic, as shown in Figure 5.4. Now the two graphics have a better balance on the slide.

Now it's time to manage the awkward break in the title of Slide 5.

13. Scroll down to display Slide 5 in Normal view.

14. Click in the title to place your insertion point after the word Traffic.

15. Press Shift+Enter. Now the title breaks in a more acceptable way (no longer dangling one lone word on a second line).

You have to update the two summary slides to reflect the final content of your presentation. Do that now by first deleting the antiquated slides, and inserting a new summary slide.

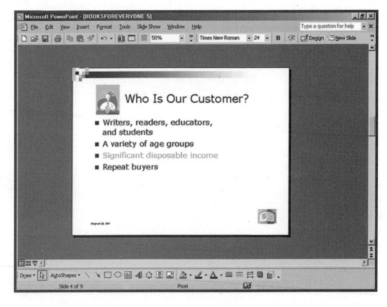

Figure 5.4

Placeholder positions can be changed on the Slide Master for all slides, or on individual slides for unique positioning.

16. If the Outline pane isn't on-screen, select View, Normal (Restore Panes) and click on the Outline tab.

17. Select the summary slide near the top of the presentation outline.

18. Select Edit, Cut.

19. Repeat the last two steps for the summary slide at the bottom of the outline. The two slides have disappeared from the outline and appear on the Windows Clipboard pane that appears on the right, as shown in Figure 5.5. The Clipboard allows you to easily retrieve items you've placed there.

20. Click the Collapse All button on the Outlining toolbar.

21. Click and drag to select all the slide titles from Slide 2 on.

22. Click the Summary Slide button on the Outlining toolbar. A summary slide is inserted, and the Slide Layout pane is displayed automatically.

23. Display the Slide Sorter view by clicking on that icon in the bottom-left corner of PowerPoint.

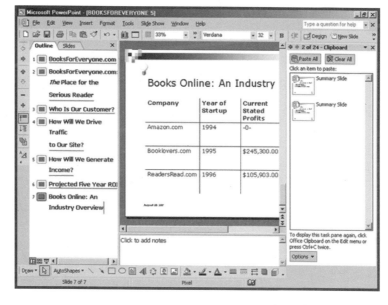

Figure 5.5

The Clipboard feature allows multiple items in more recent versions of Windows.

24. Select the summary slide and click the Copy tool on the Standard toolbar.

25. Click to place your insertion point after the last slide in the presentation, and click the Paste button on the Standard toolbar to place a copy of the summary slide at the end of the presentation.

Now review your presentation with the changes you made one more time. Things should look tidy—with all words spelled correctly—and any design inconsistencies have vanished. Now you're ready to set up how your slide show will run when you present it.

ON YOUR OWN

You need to take the time to review your real-world presentation for the same types of issues you addressed above, including:

⚙ Proper use of fonts. (Don't use too many fonts in one presentation.)

⚙ Good design on slides, making sure graphics and text form a comfortable balance on each slide.

⚙ Mechanics such as spelling, grammar, and use of punctuation.

⚙ Consistency of case: Do your bullet points use an initial capital only, or are all words capitalized? Is your use of this consistent on every slide?

Be sure to make changes to global issues—graphics or text that should appear on every slide, formatting, placeholder placement, and so on—on the Slide Master. Make changes unique to individual slides on those slides in Normal view.

Setting Up Your Slide Show

You need to make several settings before giving your PowerPoint presentation in front of an audience. Some settings control when slides change or whether a presentation should repeat itself continuously, for example. Other settings establish effects that occur when one slide goes away and a new slide appears. If you're accustomed to traditional slide shows where all you can do is click to advance to the next slide, you'll be impressed with the control PowerPoint gives you over your slide presentations.

Making General Settings for Your Show

Slide-show settings in PowerPoint give you control over how your show will run, but first you have to be sure about some variables concerning your presentation. Will the presentation be given to support a speaker, or will it be run on a computer at a trade show kiosk, continuously showing the same slides over and over again? Do you want to manually move slides forward or have them move on their own after a certain interval of time? Perhaps you only want to show the first half of the presentation, or you intend to use more than one monitor to display the slide show. Consider how, when, and where you want the presentation to happen, and then you can make the following settings.

For the purposes of our sample presentation, let's assume that it will be given by a live presenter who wants to control it manually. Take a look at where you control those settings in the Set Up Show dialog box, shown in Figure 5.6. Select Slide Show, Set Up Show to display it.

Here's what you can control in this dialog box:

✿ Show type concerns whether the presentation will be made by a speaker or will stand alone. The first option here is the standard slide show with a speaker advancing slides manually or with preset timings; the second choice shows the slides in a standard window with menus and commands provided to allow viewers to browse

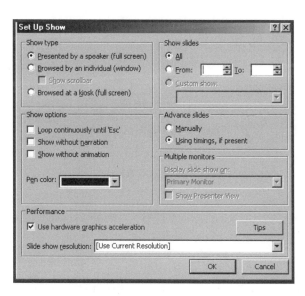

Figure 5.6

Think of setting up your slide show as a kind of technical dress rehearsal, getting all your ducks in a row before you get up in front of your audience.

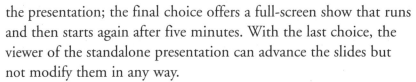

the presentation; the final choice offers a full-screen show that runs and then starts again after five minutes. With the last choice, the viewer of the standalone presentation can advance the slides but not modify them in any way.

✿ Show options control whether a show will loop (go back and start at the beginning every time it ends) and whether any recorded narration should be played. In addition, here's where you can set the color of the pen that a presenter can use to make notations on slides during the show.

✿ Show slides allows you to designate only a range of contiguous slides to include in the presentation. If you build a presentation on company benefits, for example, you might have three slides on stock options. It is logical to exclude these from the presentation when showing it to the administrative staff rather than senior management. You make that adjustment in this dialog box by entering a slide range that excludes the last three slides.

CREATING CUSTOM SHOWS

If you want more control over which slides are used in the presentation, you can select Slide Show, Custom Show and enter specific slides to include in the show. This feature allows you to use non-contiguous slides (such as Slides 1, 5, 9, and 20). You then select your custom show from the list on the Set Up Show dialog box.

Because you add slides to a custom show one at a time from a list of all slides in the presentation, you can also change the order of your slides, placing slides 1, 5, 9, then 3, 4, 11, and so on. Again, once you have created any custom show, you can set it to run from the Set Up Show dialog box. You can create as many custom shows as you like. The Custom Show feature allows you to create larger presentations and then run various versions of it with only a few quick settings.

- Advance slides has two simple settings: You can advance slides manually with a mouse click or keyboard command, or if you set timings for slides, (which you'll do later) choosing the Using timings options here lets the preset timings control the advance of slides. This setting is used most often in standalone presentations.

- Multiple monitors is available only if you have video cards set up on your computer. For example, if you want to see your notes on your monitor while your slide show is displayed on another for your viewers, you'd select which monitor should display your slide show.

- Performance controls speed and resolution issues. If your computer has a hardware graphics accelerator installed, checking that option might give some improvement in speed for your presentation. Also, if your computer uses a very high screen resolution, you might want to change the Slide show resolution to be less fine. That's because a lower setting here can make your playback of slides faster.

To show the entire slide show with a speaker present and timings overriding manual advances, you don't need to change any settings in this dialog box, so you can click OK to close it now, accepting its default settings. However, it is always a good idea to check these settings before each presentation, because any changes to the default settings will be saved with the file.

Applying Transitions

Transitions are effects that occur in the moment when one slide disappears and another appears in your slide show. Transitions control how your new slide will appear: with a special effect such as the appearance of flying in from one side of the screen or as an eight-spoke wheel entering the screen clockwise. Some of these transitions can help your slides make a pretty grand entrance. You can work with transitions from either Normal or Slide Sorter view:

1. With Slide Sorter view displayed, click on the first slide in the presentation, and holding down the Shift key, click on the last slide to select all slides.

2. Select Slide Show, Slide Transition. The Slide Transition pane shown in Figure 5.7 appears.

3. Click on the transition called Newsflash in the Apply to Selected Slides list. The effect previews on all the slides in your presentation. It's cute but perhaps too flashy for this presentation to potential investors.

TIP

If you want to apply different transition effects in different areas of your presentation, simply select each set of slides, and apply transitions to them separately. Another option is to apply the Random Transition option in the Apply to Selected Slides list; this randomly changes the transitions used to provide the greatest variety.

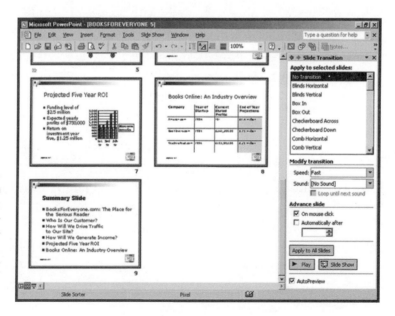

Figure 5.7

Here's where you determine whether your slides enter with a stripe, circular, or downward motion, among others.

4. Select the transition called Shape Diamond from the list of transitions. The effect previews: attention-getting but not too glitzy.

5. Click on the arrow in the Speed field and select Medium to have the effect play more slowly.

6. Save the presentation.

NOTE If you want to set slides to advance after an increment of time, you can do that in the Slide Transition pane by checking the Automatically After checkbox, and entering a number of minutes or seconds in the Advance slide area.

Using Animation Schemes

How slides appear on your screen when they're first displayed isn't the only thing you can control in your slide show; you can also control how individual text elements appear. If you like, you can set one or more slides to display the title and bullet points one at a time, for example. Try that now with your initial summary slide:

1. Click on the first summary slide to select it.

2. Select Slide Show, Animation Schemes. The Slide Design pane appears with animation schemes displayed, as shown in Figure 5.8.

3. Click on the animation called Fade in one by one; it previews on the summary slide in Slide Sorter view.

4. Save the presentation.

You can apply animation schemes to every slide in your presentation or only the slides you have selected when you apply a scheme.

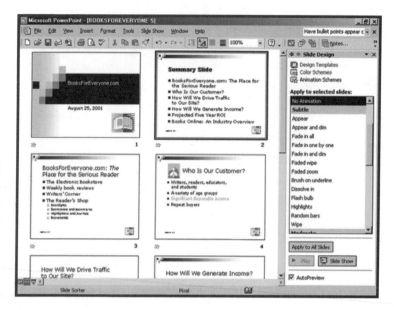

Figure 5.8

Here's the Slide Design pane you saw when working with design templates, but now it displays animation design choices.

Recording a Narration

If you can't show up for your own presentation, you might want to record a narration to accompany it. You can record a narration and arrange for the narration and your slides to be displayed in sync with preset timing, or you can include a narration that plays with each slide as it appears under your manual control.

You can use narrations not only to provide a speaker when one can't be present, but also to bring other speakers to your presentation: as in a greeting for the audience from your CEO that plays on the first slide of your presentation and enthusiastic customer testimonials on another slide.

To record a narration, first you must have a sound card installed on your computer, and microphone connected to your computer; then, follow these steps:

1. Select Slide Show, Record Narration. The dialog box in Figure 5.9 appears.

Figure 5.9

If you have narrations in another presentation, you can easily add them to this one by selecting the Link Narrations In checkbox

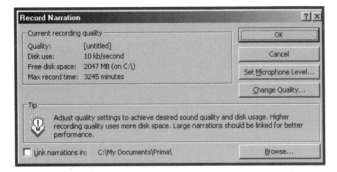

 **CAUTION** If you link to a narration file in another presentation, be careful. When you take your presentation on the road, if you don't also bring that other presentation with you, stored in the presentation folder, PowerPoint won't be able to play it.

2. Click on Set Microphone Level. This produces a dialog box with a bit of text for you to read.

3. Read the text; as you do so, the Microphone Setup Wizard from Windows displays a readout to show whether your microphone is working.

4. When you're done reading, click on OK to return to the Record Narration dialog box.

5. Click on OK to initiate the narration recording. A dialog box appears asking whether you want to start the narration on the currently selected slide or the first slide.

6. Click on First Slide.

7. The first slide in your presentation appears in Slide Show view. Read this text into your microphone:

   "Welcome to the BooksForEveryone.com investors' presentation. We are excited to have this opportunity to tell you about our Internet startup venture."

8. Press the right-arrow key on your keyboard; the presentation advances one slide.

9. Read the following:

   "During this presentation, I will give you an overview of what BooksForEveryone.com is all about and what our goals and vision are. I will examine who our potential customers are and how we will locate those customers and bring them to our site to use content and make purchases. We will also discuss how we will generate income in a variety of creative ways and review a projected five-year return-on-investment scenario. Finally, I will provide an overview of what the book and reader community is doing online today."

10. When you're done reading, press Escape. The slide show stops, and the dialog box in Figure 5.10 appears. Although the narrations themselves have already been saved, if you want to save the timing that you used to read the narration and change to the next slide along with the narration, you have to do that here.

11. Click on Save to save the timing with the narrations. You return to Slide Sorter view.

12. Select the first slide in your presentation and then switch to Slide Show by clicking that icon on the bottom-left corner of PowerPoint's screen.

Figure 5.10

This is where you can coordinate your narration with the timing of slides.

Microsoft PowerPoint	✕
ⓘ The narrations have been saved with each slide. Do you want to save the slide timings as well?	
[Save] [Don't Save]	

TIP You can always play your slide show from the beginning no matter which slide is selected by pressing F5.

13. Watch the presentation, listening to the narration you recorded for the first two slides. Press Escape when the narration has finished to leave the slide show.

14. Save the file.

That's all that you have to do to record a narration. Remember, if you don't want to play the narration at a particular presentation of this slide show, you can select Slide Show, Set Up Show, and select Show Without Narration from the Set Up Show dialog box.

Running a Slide Show

You might not know it, but when you started learning PowerPoint, you wandered into the world of show business. Although some presentations are played on their own at kiosks or published on the Web, a great many are presented with a speaker. Sometimes, that speaker will be you, which makes you the star of the show.

Once you have made the slide-show settings covered earlier, you should practice running through your show a few times. You should also make any preparations you need if you're taking your show on the road, such as verifying the display equipment that you will be using and checking whether PowerPoint is installed on the presentation computer.

Navigating a Show

You know what they say: How do you get to Broadway? Practice, practice, practice. That's good advice for a PowerPoint presenter as well. The more familiar you are with your content, slide sequence, and multimedia effects, the more relaxed you can be during your presentation.

Try running through the BooksForEveryone slide show now:

1. Open BooksForEveryone5.
2. Select Slide Show, Set Up Show, and click in the Show Without Narration checkbox. You can suppress a recorded narration in this way when you are going to give a presentation in person.
3. Click OK to close the dialog box.
4. Begin the slide show by pressing F5. The first slide appears full screen.

You now have several options for moving through your presentation. To simply move from slide to slide in order, you can use the right- and left-arrow keys on your keyboard to move to the next and previous slide, respectively. The Up and Down arrows and Page Up and Page Down arrows perform the same functions (up for previous, down for next). You can also click your mouse to move forward one slide.

Another way to move around is to use the commands on the shortcut menu available in Slide Show, shown in Figure 5.11. Because this displays a pop-up menu, it's not the method to use to move through your presentation sequentially. However, if you want to jump to a slide elsewhere in your presentation, it provides a quicker method. You access this menu by clicking on the navigation button in the bottom-left corner of the slide or right-clicking anywhere in your presentation.

TIP If the navigation button and shortcut menu aren't available, somebody may have changed the setting for how these operate by default in your Options dialog box. Select Tools, Options, and display the View tab of the dialog box. Then check the settings in the Slide Show section of this dialog box.

Figure 5.11

This menu offers commands for moving around your presentation, as well as presenter's tools for making notes.

●●

NOTE PowerPoint also offers an action button feature that can help you navigate either within your presentation or to other documents, such as a Web page. You can select Slide Show, Action Button to select one of several styles of buttons to place on your slide. Actions are already associated with that button: such as jumping to a Web link or another slide in the presentation.

●●

From the shortcut menu, you can choose the Next or Previous commands to go forward or back by one slide. You can also choose the Go command; from the side menu that appears, you can then select Slide Navigator, which displays the dialog box shown in Figure 5.12, or By Title. Slide Navigator lists all the slides in the presentation, along with a notation of the last slide you displayed. Click on a slide title and then on Go To to jump to that slide. The By Title command doesn't display a dialog box; rather, it displays an additional side-menu listing of all the slides in the presentation. This is almost identical to the Slide Navigator function except that you click on a slide name in the side menu and immediately go to it.

Figure 5.12

Slide Navigator offers two things By Title doesn't: the option of seeing a custom show (a subset of slides) and an indication of the last slide viewed.

Finally, you can use several additional keyboard shortcuts while in the slide show. These are listed in Table 5.1.

TIP

While displaying a slide show, you can press F1 to access a Help menu that lists all keystroke shortcuts.

Working with Presenter's Tools

When you looked at the navigation button menu in Figure 5.11, you may have noticed several more options above and beyond simple navigation tools. Specifically, you saw Meeting Minder, Speaker Notes, Pointer Options, and Screen commands. These are presenter's tools; you can use them in the following ways:

- Meeting Minder allows you to take minutes of a presentation and set action items for later follow-up. You can read minutes you take during a show by selecting Tools, Meeting Minder.

- Speaker Notes allows you to add speaker notes while rehearsing a presentation.

TABLE 5.1 SLIDE-SHOW KEYBOARD SHORTCUTS	
Keys	**Results**
N, Enter, Spacebar	Move to next slide (or initiate the next animation if you have more than one on a slide).
P, Page Up, Backspace	Move to the previous animation or slide.
slide number+Enter	Go to the specified slide number.
B, . (period)	Show a black screen; hide a black screen and return to the show.
W, , (comma)	Show a white screen; hide a white screen and return to the show.
S, + (plus sign)	Stop or restart a slide show set to run automatically.
Esc, Ctrl+Break, - (hyphen)	Close slide show.
E	Erase onscreen notations.
H	Go to the next hidden slide.
T	Change timings while rehearsing your show.
O	Use original timings.
M	Set the show to advance on mouse click.
Ctrl+P	Display a pointer that's hidden; change the pointer to a pen.
Ctrl+A	Display a pointer that's hidden; change the pointer to an arrow.
Ctrl+H	Hide both pointer and navigation button right away.
Ctrl+U	Hide both pointer and navigation button in 15 seconds.
Shift+F10	Show shortcut menu.
Tab	Go to the next hyperlink.
Shift+Tab	Go to the last hyperlink.

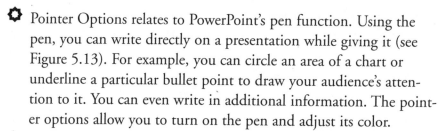

● Pointer Options relates to PowerPoint's pen function. Using the pen, you can write directly on a presentation while giving it (see Figure 5.13). For example, you can circle an area of a chart or underline a particular bullet point to draw your audience's attention to it. You can even write in additional information. The pointer options allow you to turn on the pen and adjust its color.

● Screen allows you to pause the presentation, erase pen marks on a slide, or go to a black screen, which you might want to do if you're taking a long pause in your presentation to explain a concept or you want to take a short break.

Take the time now to move through your presentation, viewing any animations or special effects and practicing with the pen and adding meeting minutes. Try using several of the methods of navigation described earlier.

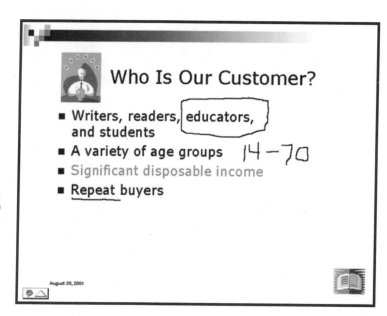

Figure 5.13

The PowerPoint pen is a handy way to add information while presenting or draw attention to a point.

Rehearsing Timing

One of the important aspects of giving a live presentation is timing. A presenter is typically given a set period of time to talk, and he or she must be comfortable that the information in the presentation can be covered within that timeframe. Also, a presenter must pace a presentation so the audience is kept interested and all the material can be covered appropriately.

You can use the Rehearse Timings feature to practice your presentation timing before an in-person presentation, or add timings to control the display of slides in a standalone presentation. This feature turns on a timer, shown in Figure 5.14, which tallies the total time it takes you to move through a slide-show presentation. When you finish the presentation, you are also offered the option of saving the timing you used to display each slide. When you do, if you have set your slide show (Slide Show, Set Up Show) to use Timings if present, the slides advance automatically according to the timing you save here.

To rehearse your timings, follow these steps:

1. Display the first slide in the presentation in Normal view (or select the first slide in Slide Sorter view).

2. Select Slide Show, Rehearse Timings. PowerPoint goes into Slide Show mode, and a small dialog box displays a counter reflecting the seconds that your slides are displayed.

3. Move through the show, taking the time to read each bullet point on the slide before you move forward.

Figure 5.14

This timer records total presentation time, as well as the time that each slide is displayed.

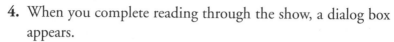

4. When you complete reading through the show, a dialog box appears.

5. Click on Yes to save the slide timings.

6. Change to Slide Sorter view and note the individual slide timings now associated with each slide, as shown in Figure 5.15.

7. Save the presentation.

Taking Your Show on the Road

You should do a few things to prepare to give a PowerPoint presentation away from your office. First, you should ascertain whether the computer you are using for the presentation has PowerPoint loaded on it. If it doesn't, you have to provide the PowerPoint Viewer. The Viewer allows you to run a presentation even if PowerPoint isn't available. You can download the viewer for free from Microsoft's Download Web site (**http://www.microsoft.com/downloads**). The Viewer is also on the CD included with this book.

Figure 5.15

If a show is running long or short, review these timings to see where you're spending too much—or too little—time on a topic.

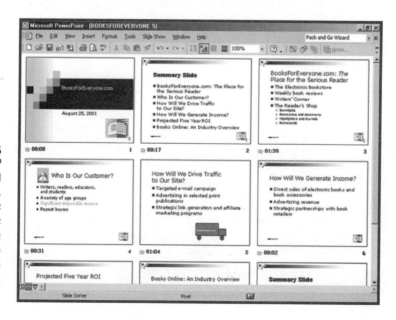

◆ ◆

CAUTION Some features in PowerPoint 2002 aren't supported by the Viewer, including animations, ActiveX controls, and transparency levels. In addition, the Viewer won't open any presentation that you have password-protected. If you are relying on the Viewer to play your presentation, run through the show several times beforehand to check for problems.

◆ ◆

You can save the Viewer with your presentation by using the Pack and Go Wizard, shown in Figure 5.16. You run the wizard by selecting File, Pack and Go Wizard. You can then move through several forms and make choices, including choosing the presentation you want to pack, selecting a destination for it (for example, a floppy disk), indicating whether you want all files hyperlinked to the presentation to be saved with it, and choosing to include the Viewer with the presentation.

If you've downloaded the viewer, you see the option of including it in the Viewer portion of the wizard; if you haven't, you can use the button on that form, shown in Figure 5.17, to download it.

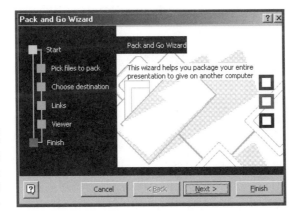

Figure 5.16

The wizard makes it easy to save a presentation for the road.

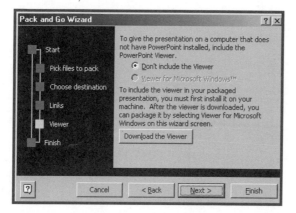

Figure 5.17

If you know the computer you'll be using to give your presentation doesn't have PowerPoint loaded, be sure to bring the Viewer with you!

◆◆

CAUTION Several variables could come up when you give a presentation from a different computer; for example, even if you select to embed TrueType fonts in a packed presentation, some of those fonts are copyrighted and won't be available for that reason. In addition, the display equipment might not display colors quite the way your own computer did. Always leave time to run through a presentation on site, if at all possible, to find and fix these problems before the audience shows up.

◆◆

Publishing Your Presentation to the Web

The World Wide Web has provided a perfect place for sharing presentations, and PowerPoint has kept up with the times by including several online presentation options:

- ♦ You can save a file as a Web archive and post that file on a Web site. For example, you can place an archive version of your presentation on your Team Web Site where people with access can view it.

- ♦ You can publish a presentation to the Web; using this approach, you create a Web page and control some of the settings for showing the presentation.

✪ You can set up a live broadcast of a presentation on your company network. You can include audio and video in a broadcast presentation (but you must have a video camera and a microphone attached to your computer to use these two features).

Saving Your Presentation as a Web Page

The simplest way to make your presentation available to others in Web page format is to save it as a Web archive and then email or give the file to someone on a floppy disk. A Web archive contains all the elements of your presentation in a MIME aggregate HTML document, known as MHTML. What this means is that a person can display the presentation in a Web browser by simply double-clicking on the file. The presentation includes its own navigation tools.

To save a file as a Web archive, follow these steps:

1. Open the file you want to save.
2. Select File, Save as Web Page.
3. In the Save As dialog box shown in Figure 5.18, provide a name for the presentation and a location to save it to.
4. Change the Save As Type setting to Web Archive.
5. Click Save to save the file.

To play the file, locate it with Windows Explorer, and double-click on it. It opens in your default browser with a slide list and simple navigation tools that allow you to move through the presentation. There is also a button you can click to show the presentation in full screen, as in a traditional slide show, and another to add notes to the presentation.

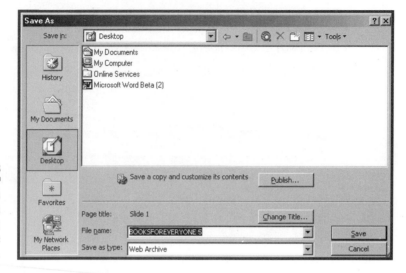

Figure 5.18

You can save a presentation as a Web page through the familiar Save As dialog box.

CAUTION Because PowerPoint is a Microsoft product, it has made Web versions of presentations display optimally when you use Microsoft's browser, Internet Explorer. Although when publishing a presentation to the Web you can make settings that optimize your presentation for Netscape Navigator, you still lose some key features, such as sound and movies. My advice: Suggest to anyone viewing your Web archive or published presentation that she download and view it in Internet Explorer 4.0 or later.

Publishing a Presentation to the Web

When you publish a presentation to the Web, you can make viewing settings that you don't have access to when you simply save the file as a Web archive.

You can see these settings by walking through the publish procedure:

1. With BooksForEveryone5 displayed, select File, Save As Web Page.

2. In the Save As dialog box, click on Publish. The dialog box shown in Figure 5.19 appears.

Figure 5.19

Control how your presentation will look and run online from this dialog box.

Here's what you can control in this dialog box:

- You can designate that you want to publish the complete presentation, only a subset of contiguous slides, or a custom show. Custom shows must be created prior to opening this dialog box for them to be available.

- You can choose to display or not display speaker notes. If you choose to display them, they will be visible to anybody viewing your Web presentation, so be sure that their content is appropriate to a general audience.

- You can indicate which browsers you believe will be used to view the presentation; if you select something other than Internet Explorer 4.0 and later, PowerPoint optimizes the presentation for other browsers, but be aware that some features of your presentation may be lost. Unless you are publishing your Web page to a closed computing environment, for example a company intranet where everybody uses Internet Explorer as their browser, you should assume other browsers will be used to view it.

✪ You can designate a file name and indicate that the presentation should be opened in your browser when you complete the Publish operation. Take care that the file name you designate here is a logical one by which the viewer of your show can identify it.

In addition, you can click on the Web Options button in this dialog box to make these changes:

✪ Select a checkbox to display navigation controls along with your presentation.

✪ You can set up how browsers will deal with your presentation by designating that the browser should be allowed to resize slides to fit the browser window or choosing whether the browser will play animations that appear in your presentation.

✪ Control file names and links for Web page presentations including use of long file names and how files and links are organized in a single folder for the presentation. It's a good idea to check these settings, so no linked files go missing from your Web presentation.

✪ You can set the screen resolution for the target monitor. It's a good idea to set this for the average user's monitor; 800x600 is usually safe for most Web users today.

✪ Choose a font set for your presentation; typically you will choose English/Western European for this, but several other language sets are available.

When you've made appropriate settings for your presentation and audience, click on Publish.

Broadcasting a Presentation

Presentation broadcasting provides a method for giving a live presentation over the Web, including audio and video. You can schedule a broadcast using Outlook or another email program; you can also save a broadcast and provide it for people to view at their leisure. Broadcasting a presentation is a great way to save time and money because people

don't have to travel to a meeting. It allows you to provide a close to in-person support of your slides. However, it does lack some of the energy of an in-person interaction, where a speaker can pick up on audience reactions and accept questions about the presentation content during the presentation. In addition, at this point the process of setting up and viewing a broadcast is a bit complicated, and holds the potential for technical glitches.

The viewer of a broadcast presentation needs a Web browser; the broadcaster needs a video camera and microphone if audio and video are to be included. Also, to broadcast a presentation, you must have Internet Explorer 5.1 or later and access to a Windows Media Server.

TIP To learn about how to set up your microphone and video camera with your computer, check your documentation for this equipment or contact the equipment manufacturer.

Setting Up a Broadcast

You can set several variables for broadcasting a presentation, depending on the location of your Windows Media Server, whether you want to save the presentation as it's being given, whether you have the equipment to use audio or video, and so on.

Because of these variables, and because you may or may not be connected to a network server as you work through this book this weekend, I don't take you through the process step by step. However, I've provided the basic procedure to start a broadcast.

Begin by selecting Slide Show, Online Broadcast, Start Live Broadcast Now. The Live Presentation Broadcast dialog box shown in Figure 5.21 appears. In this dialog box, you can essentially designate whether you want to record the presentation; then, click Broadcast to continue.

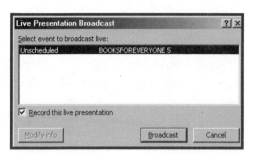

Figure 5.21

This is the first step in generating any live broadcast.

The Live Presentation Broadcast dialog box that appears next (see Figure 5.22) lets you enter information about your presentation; this information is displayed when someone "arrives" at your live broadcast in an area called the Lobby. This dialog box is also where you access settings for your broadcast.

To make settings for the presentation, click on the Settings button on the Live Presentation Broadcast dialog box. This displays the Broadcast Settings dialog box shown in Figure 5.23. You decide whether the presentation will use audio or video, and you designate a server location and a chat room associated with the presentation.

When you've made all the settings that reflect your server and audio/video setup, you can click OK to close that dialog box, then click Start from the Live Presentation Broadcast dialog box to begin the presentation.

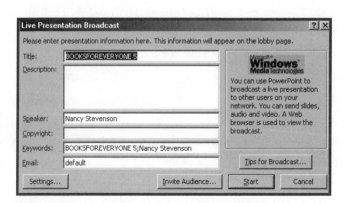

Figure 5.22

Provide a brief description of your topic and contents by entering it in this dialog box.

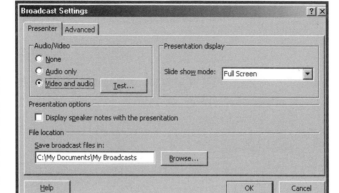

Figure 5.23

You can pick options for the audio and video, presentation display, and server on the tabs of this dialog box.

TIP If you want to record a broadcast presentation that you will never present live, you can select Slide Show, Online Broadcast, Record and Save Broadcast.

What's Next?

What's next? You're going to take what you've learned this weekend and use it on real-world presentations; that practice will help you retain everything you've learned. You'll meet your current presentation deadline and impress your boss. And as you work through presentations in the future, you'll explore some of the more sophisticated tools of PowerPoint, many of which are referenced in this book. It's my hope that the understanding you've gained this weekend of how PowerPoint is organized, the presentation terms and concepts, and PowerPoint tools gives you a solid foundation for becoming a PowerPoint pro. Good luck!

Great Presentations Idea Gallery

Sometimes it's hard to get your creative juices flowing. When you're having a hard time generating ideas for your presentation, take a look at the work of others. You'll find good ideas in many places. Co-workers and associates are a great source of inspiration. These people can sit down and have a brainstorming session with you or share presentations that they've created. Another place to look is on the Internet and in PowerPoint newsgroups. You'll find examples of presentations and a ton of good advice. Television and movies can inspire you in ways that you might not realize. The professionals have large creative staffs and budgets to match. Try your hand at reproducing some of the effects they produce to give your presentation a professional touch.

The presentation gallery and the CD included with this book are other sources of ideas. The presentations in this gallery show that you don't need a lot of time, an enormous budget, or extensive experience as a graphic designer to create well-designed and effective presentations.

A Speaker-Driven Presentation

The most common way to present a slide show is to use a speaker to deliver the presentation and control the transition from one slide to another. An example of a speaker-driven presentation appears in the file freedive.pps, which is located in the examples/pressie1 folder on the CD-ROM. This presentation was saved as a PowerPoint show so that the presenter could easily put the presentation on a diskette, travel around the country, and show the presentation on any available computer. To start this show, double-click on the filename. To move from slide to slide, click on a slide or press the right-arrow key.

This presentation uses the following PowerPoint features:

* The background for Slides 1 through 4 uses the Ocean design template applied to the slide master. A logo was also added to the slide master so it would appear on Slides 2 through 4. A duplicate was made of the slide master so that the logo would not appear on Slide 5.

* The background for Slide 5 is a scanned photograph saved in JPEG format. The background was applied to the slide, and the background graphics were omitted from the slide master.

* The list items were formatted using a Webdings symbol as the bullet character.

Figure A.1

✪ Slides 3 and 4 use a custom animation that plays automatically when the slide appears during the show.

✪ The slide show was set up to be presented by a speaker and to advance slides manually. The slide show appears as a full-screen presentation.

✪ The file was saved as a PowerPoint show, and the TrueType fonts (for those characters used in the presentation) were embedded in the file.

TIP Animations do not perform in the same way on every computer, and you might find that an animation does not run smoothly. Because an animation takes a specific amount of time to complete, slower computers need to skip steps to stay within the animation timeframe. To reduce jerkiness on slower computers, use lower-resolution pictures, make the physical size of the picture smaller, or use a simple background on the slides.

An Educational Presentation

Another situation where a speaker can effectively utilize a slide show is when the information is educational in nature, as in the presentation named chicken.ppt, which is located in the examples/pressie2 folder on the CD-ROM. When you use words and pictures together, you can have a greater impact on your audience, and they will have an easier time remembering the information presented. Notes and handouts are effective in educational presentations. Notes help the speaker stay on track, and handouts help the audience recall the presentation for later use.

This presentation uses the following PowerPoint features:

⚙ The background for all the slides uses the Profile design template.

⚙ The slide show starts with a slide transition and a sound effect on Slide 1. Slides 2 through 4 use the same slide-transition effect.

⚙ Speaker notes help the lecturer deliver the presentation and create handouts so that the audience can recall the information delivered in the presentation.

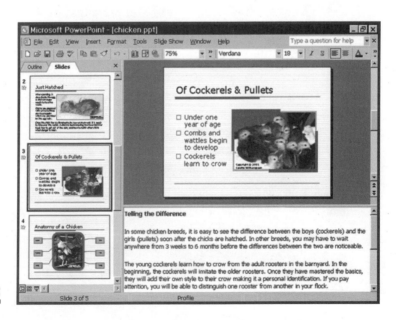

Figure A.2

- Photographs were scanned at print quality (200 dpi) using the Microsoft Office Document Imaging feature. AutoShapes were used to create a frame around the photographs in Slides 3 and 4.

- On Slide 4, AutoShapes are used as callouts to help identify different parts of a picture.

- Slide 5 uses an animation effect to display text on screen. You'll also hear a sound during the animation.

- The slide show is set up to be delivered by a speaker using manual timings. When you open the file, the presentation appears in PowerPoint (so that you can read the notes). To play the show, press the F5 key.

A Photo Album

When you are looking for a way to share photographs from your vacation or to showcase your artwork, try the Photo Album feature. The Photo Album makes it easy to organize and catalog a group of photographs or other types of pictures. You can even add captions and text boxes that describe and enhance each picture. The Photo Album keeps a list of the pictures and text boxes in the presentation so that you can easily rearrange pictures, add new pictures, and delete existing pictures. The Photo Album showcased in the file album.pps (located on the CD under examples/pressie3) is an example of how you can share your vacation memories with friends and relatives.

 NOTE PowerPoint creates photo albums in a new file; the photo album is not added to an existing file. To start a photo album, click on Insert, Picture, New Photo Album to open the Photo Album dialog box. Use the dialog box to add pictures to the album and create placeholders for text boxes.

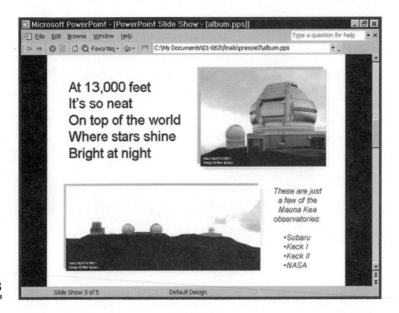

Figure A.3

This presentation uses the following PowerPoint features:

- The photo album uses the 4 pictures Picture layout option which creates slides that contain four placeholders (that can contain either pictures or text boxes). Each slide has two photos and two text boxes. The photo album does not use captions below the photographs.

- Photographs were inserted from a scanner, and a beveled effect was added to each photograph. The photographs were scanned at screen/Web quality.

- The background uses a two-color gradient applied to the slide master.

- The slide show was set up to be browsed by an individual in a separate window and uses manual timings.

- The file is saved as a PowerPoint show and opens in a viewer window. To see how this presentation was developed, start PowerPoint and open the file from PowerPoint. Select Format, Photo Album to display the album content.

Web Graphics

PowerPoint has the ability to convert slides into GIF or JPEG format so you can use slides as graphics in Web pages. You can use clip art, art created by a graphics software application, scanned photographs, and AutoShapes on slides that will be converted to a Web-compatible file format. These converted slides can then be used when designing Web pages in an HTML editor, such as FrontPage. The file named imagemap.ppt (located on the CD under examples/pressie4) is an example of artwork used as the background for an image map created in FrontPage. The presentation slide was saved in JPEG format to produce the file named imagemap.jpg and then inserted in a Web page created in FrontPage. FrontPage was then used to create the image map hotspots and associated hyperlinks. The result appears in the file named kidsites.htm. Open this Web page in a Web browser, hold the mouse pointer over each of the images to see the screen tip, and then click on an image to visit the associated Web site.

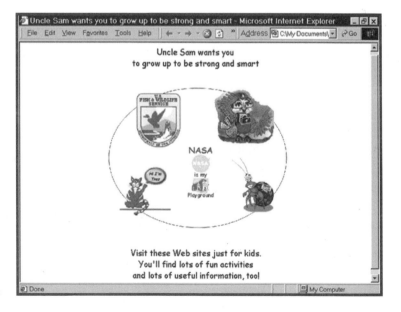

Figure A.4

This presentation uses the following PowerPoint features:

- The images used as hotspots were inserted from a file, and the background is an AutoShape that uses a fill color and a line color.
- The pictures were then compressed (at Web/screen resolution) using the Compress Pictures tool on the Picture toolbar.
- The file was saved from PowerPoint in JPEG format using the Save As Web Page feature. FrontPage can only make image maps if an image is in GIF or JPEG format.

TIP   You can also use the GIF format for Web graphics, but it might give you an image of unacceptable quality. If you find that slides become speckled when converted to GIF, use the JPEG format.

Online Presentations

Sometimes your presentation needs to do double, or even triple, duty. You might need a presentation that you can use as a slide show and also publish to a Web site. Although you might not think of PowerPoint as a Web site creation and design tool, it proves itself very capable in these situations. Two examples of a dual-duty presentation are the online resumes in resume1.htm and resume2.htm. These two online resumes are identical except that each takes a different navigation control approach. To open these files, double-click on the filename to display the files in your default Web browser.

NOTE   To learn more about creating Web-based slide-show presentations, turn to Appendix B, "Ten Steps to an Effective Web Presentation."

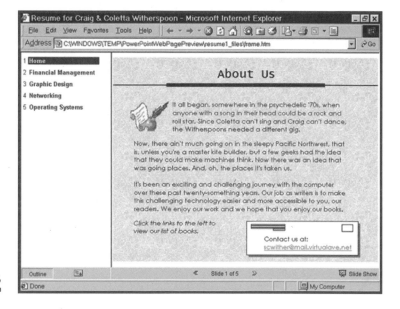

Figure A.5

The presentation named resume1.htm uses these PowerPoint features:

- The original file was created as a standard PowerPoint file (using the .ppt file format), and when the presentation was finished, it was saved as a Web page.

- The Web page was set up using the presentation outline as the navigation control.

- The background uses the blue tissue-paper texture fill effect and was applied to the slide master.

- GIF images were inserted on the slides, and then the Compress Pictures feature was used to decrease download time.

The presentation named resume2.htm uses these PowerPoint features:

- The original file was created as a PowerPoint presentation file and saved as a Web page.

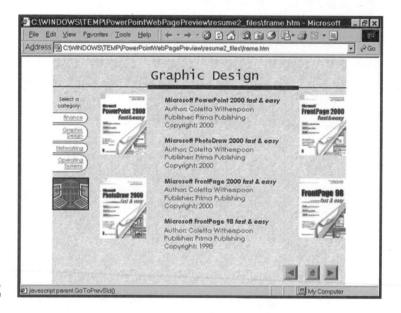

Figure A.6

○ The navigation controls were created on the slide master. The navigation bar along the left edge uses hyperlinks to link to the individual slides. Action buttons appear at the bottom-right corner so the visitor can easily move from one slide to the next.

○ An animated GIF was added to the slide master to give movement to the slides.

Movie Credits

The coolest new feature of PowerPoint is the collection of animation effects you can apply to text and images. You'll be amazed by the number of animation effects in which text and images can appear on a slide, dance around, and slide off the screen. These effects make PowerPoint the perfect tool for the amateur and home videographer. If you insert a movie in a presentation and add animated titles and credits, your friends will wonder when you plan that big move to Hollywood. Although the file cruise.pps, which is located in the examples/pressie7 folder on the CD-

ROM doesn't include a movie, it does show you how animation effects can provide movie-style credits that roll across the screen.

This presentation uses the following PowerPoint features:

- Each slide has a different background applied to the slide. A slide master was not used.

- The animation on Slide 1 uses the Wave emphasis effect. To create a larger wave, the motion path was modified.

- The animations on Slide 2 use several effects. The text appears on screen using the Crawl In entrance effect, changes to a contrasting color while staying in one place for a second, and then uses the Crawl Out exit effect.

- To create a self-running presentation, timings were set for each slide, and the file was saved in the PowerPoint show format.

Figure A.7

Charts, Graphs, and Tables

No presentation is complete without a few charts and graphs. Charts and graphs are an effective way to organize information when you want to get your point across quickly. Charts and graphs are a graphical way to show a relationship between different types of information. Before you start a chart or graph, gather your information and then take a look at the different options available in PowerPoint. Another way to organize information uses tables. Tables arrange information in rows and columns and provide an easy way to organize information so that it can be scanned quickly. Examples of charts, graphs, and table can be seen in the file trails.pps, which is located in the examples/pressie8 folder on the CD-ROM.

This presentation uses the following PowerPoint features:

✪ Slide 1 uses an animation effect to introduce the show.

✪ Slide 2 contains an organization chart and uses a WordArt object as a title heading.

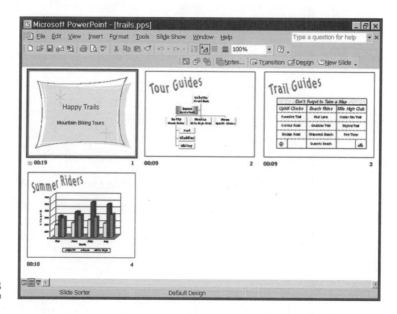

Figure A.8

⚙ Slide 3 formats information into a table to make it easier to read the contents.

⚙ Slide 4 uses a chart to show the relationship between collected data.

⚙ The slide show is set up as a self-running presentation shown at full-screen view.

APPENDIX B

Ten Steps to an Effective Web Presentation

Every application in the Microsoft Office suite has the capability to create pages that can be browsed on the Internet. You can either publish these pages directly on the Internet or include them in a Web site created in FrontPage. You can also convert PowerPoint slide-show presentations to HTML format so that they can be viewed in a Web browser. To get started on a Web-based slide show presentation, follow these ten steps.

Step 1: Learn About Good Web Design

Web site creation and design is a large and complex subject, and you need a good grounding in the basics before you create your first Web-based slide-show presentation. One of the best ways to learn how to design effective Web pages is to explore other Web sites. If you need some good advice, search the Internet for tutorials, discussion groups, how-tos, and FAQs. Or start with this Web-design recommended reading list:

- ✿ **The NCSA Beginner's Guide to HTML (http://www.ncsa.uiuc.edu/General/Internet/WWW/ HTMLPrimer.html).** This site provides a good introduction to HTML and how it is used to create Web pages.

- ✿ **MSDN Online Web Workshop (http://msdn.microsoft.com/workshop/).** The Microsoft Developer Network provides a wealth of information on various technologies involved in creating Web sites. You might want to start with the Essentials, Design, and Web Content Management sections.

- ✿ **The About Network (http://www.about.com/internet/).** The About Network hosts several Internet forums that range in topics from Internet applications to Web-page design. You might want to check out the Personal Web Pages forum for specific information on Web page design.

- ✿ **The Webmaster's Reference Library (http://www.webreference.com/).** This site is chock-full of articles about how to design effective Web sites and how to use images and multimedia on Web pages; tutorials on how to use various Web creation tools; and information on HTML.

- ✿ **Webmonkey (http://hotwired.lycos.com/webmonkey).** Webmonkey is a reference site for Web developers that contains information on authoring and designing Web pages and using multimedia on Web pages. It also contains some great projects to help children get started with Web-page development.

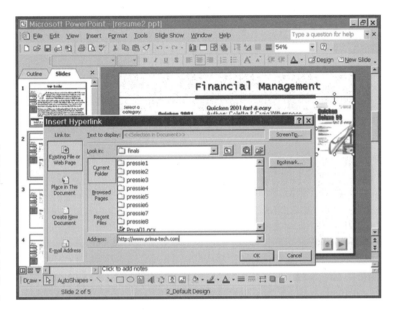

Figure B.1

It's easy to add hyperlinks to a presentation slide. Select the text or graphic that you want to use as the hyperlink and click on the Hyperlink button on the Standard toolbar.

Step 2: Plan Your Web Presentation

Just as all good business ventures start out with a business plan, a good Web presentation also needs a plan. A Web presentation needs direction, informative content, and excitement. These things keep visitors involved and eager to visit your Web site time and time again. At the base of every successful Web site is a detailed plan and a solid organization structure. Before you begin, answer the following questions:

✪ What goals do you want to achieve with your Web-based presentation?

✪ What is the theme of your presentation?

✪ What message do you want to relay to your visitors?

✪ How many slides will there be, and how will they be linked together?

✪ What type of content (such as words, pictures, and multimedia) will be included in the presentation?

⚙ Will your Web presentation be used as a standalone Web site, or will it be a part of an existing Web site?

⚙ Where will the Web presentation be published?

Step 3: Create the Web Presentation File

The best way to start a Web-based slide-show presentation is to create a PowerPoint file using the PowerPoint native file format (the .ppt extension). This gives you the flexibility of using the slide show as both a regular PowerPoint presentation and a Web presentation. It also makes it easier to update the presentation. You can start with a blank presentation, or you can use the AutoContent Wizard. If you use the AutoContent Wizard to create the presentation, you need to select a presentation type and then choose to output the presentation as a Web presentation. When you save the file, it uses the PowerPoint native file format (.ppt extension). After you finish creating the Web presentation, you need to save it to HTML format (see Step 8).

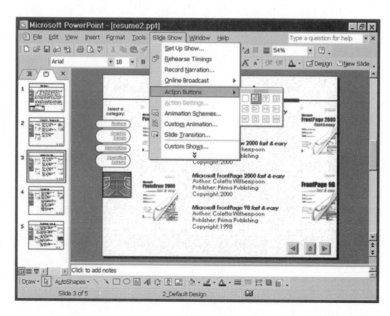

Figure B.2

To navigate between slides in a presentation, add Action Buttons to individual slides or to the slide master.

For each Web presentation you create, create a new folder in which to store the presentation and associated multimedia files. Then, collect all of the picture files, sound files, movie files, and other elements you plan to use in the presentation. (See Step 6 for a few tips about the types of media files that work.) Place these elements within the folder you created for the presentation and associated multimedia files. You want these elements in the folder before you insert them into the presentation file—to make it easier and faster for you to find files and insert them on the appropriate slides.

To see some examples of Web presentations, look at the Group Home Page presentation (shown in Figure B.3) in the AutoContent Wizard, or look at the sample Web presentations in Appendix A, "Great Presentations Idea Gallery," and the corresponding sample files on the CD-ROM.

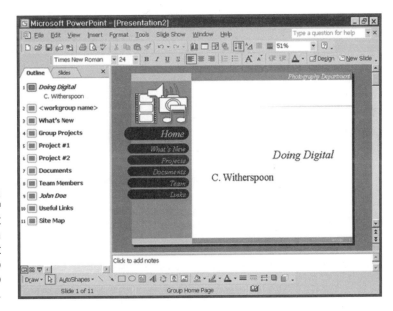

Figure B.3

PowerPoint templates contain design ideas that you are free to copy and modify to fit your needs.

Step 4: Know Your Audience

There's nothing more frustrating than going to a Web site only to find that it does not display in your browser properly. Not only is this frustrating for the visitor, but it is also frustrating for the Web designer. The cause of this frustration is the variety of Web browsers and the differences between Web browser version numbers. When designing Web pages for the Internet community, you need to consider which Web browsers your audience is using. Your visitors can be using Microsoft Internet Explorer, Netscape Navigator, Amaya, NCSA Mosaic, Lynx, a text-only browser, a hand-held organizer, or a mobile device. You'll also find that your visitors can be using any combination of browser versions—from version 3.0 to version 6.0.

How do you find out which Web browsers your visitors will be using? Well, you could conduct an informal poll of those people you know will visit your Web site. You can also fire up a browser and do some research on the Internet. Some Web sites will help you design sites for specific browsers, design sites that display well in any browser, and find statistics on browser and Web technology usage. Here are a few sites you might want to check out:

- ✪ The BrowserWatch (**http://browserwatch.internet.com/**)
- ✪ StatMarket (**http://www.statmarket.com**)
- ✪ Viewable with Any Browser Campaign (**http://www.anybrowser.org/campaign/**)

Once you've decided which browser your audience will use to view your Web-based presentation, you need to set the browser compatibility in PowerPoint:

1. Click on Tools, Options to open the Options dialog box.

2. Select the General tab and click on the Web Options button to open the Web Options dialog box.

3. Select the Browsers tab (shown in Figure B.4).

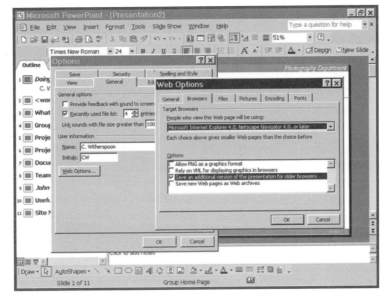

Figure B.4

Select the Web browser model and version number that is most popular with your audience.

4. Choose the browser or browsers from the People Who View This Web Page Will Be Using list box:

   ✿ If you want to reach the widest audience, select the Microsoft Internet Explorer 3.0, and Netscape Navigator 3.0, or later option. If you know that your audience uses a later version of both of these browsers, select the option for version 4.0 of both browsers.

   ✿ If you know that your audience is dedicated to the Internet Explorer browser, select one of the versions for that browser, as appropriate.

   ✿ If you're not sure what to do, selecting version 4.0 of both browsers is a pretty safe bet.

5. Click on OK to close the Web Options dialog box and the Options dialog box when you are finished.

Step 5: Develop the Presentation

A Web site is a collection of Web pages that contain text, graphics, sounds, video, and a host of other elements. Hyperlinks let visitors access the different types of elements and provide a navigation control that makes it easy for visitors to browse from one page to another. Your first consideration when building a Web site is how to create a foolproof navigation structure. Before you start developing the individual slides for your Web presentation, use these guidelines to organize your thoughts:

- ✿ **Write an outline.** All forms of written communication are easier to compose when you develop a strong outline first. An outline helps you develop good writing skills and quality content. The outline lists the major topics for inclusion in the site and shows the level of detail for coverage of those topics.

- ✿ **Draw an organization chart.** Structure a hierarchy for the individual pages. Use the outline to organize the content that will appear on each page. Decide which pages will link to which other pages in the site.

- ✿ **Create a storyboard.** Sketch a thumbnail (a small picture) of each page, showing how text should display and the positioning of pictures.

PowerPoint gives you two different options to provide a way for your audience to move from slide to slide within the presentation. You can create hyperlinks between all the slides, or you can create an outline for the presentation that can serve as a navigation control. When you use the presentation outline as a navigation control, the outline appears in one frame in the Web browser and the slide appears in another frame. Here's how to tell PowerPoint which navigation strategy to use:

1. Click on Tools, Options to open the Options dialog box.

2. Click on the General tab to display the General options.

3. Click on the Web Options button to open the Web Options dialog box.

4. Click on the General tab to display the General Web options (shown in Figure B.5).

5. If you want to use the presentation outline as a navigation control, place a checkmark in the Add Slide Navigation Controls checkbox. If you'd rather create your own hyperlinks that link the slide together, clear the checkbox.

6. When using the outline as a navigation control, select the text and background colors for the outline navigation pane from the Colors drop-down list.

7. Click on OK in the Web Options and Options dialog boxes when you are finished to close each dialog box.

Figure B.5

The navigation control converts each item in the presentation outline into a hyperlink that links to the associated slide.

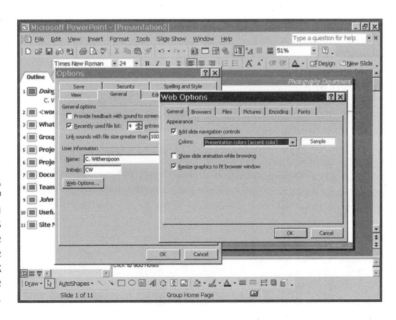

TIP

If you want to use the presentation outline as the navigation control but don't want to show the titles on each slide, drag the title placeholder off the slide. The text still shows up in the outline but is not a part of the presentation slides (an example appears in Figure B.6).

Step 6: Work with Multimedia Files

When adding multimedia files to your Web-based presentation, you need to be very careful. Multimedia files are the major cause of long download times, and not all Web browsers support all types of multimedia formats. Also, your audience may have set up their browsers so that certain multimedia elements do not download or play on their computers, or they might not have the required multimedia player installed on their systems. Other problems that can occur with multimedia files involve computer speed, video resolution, and video refresh rates. These factors can cause multimedia (especially video animations) to play slower on slower computers, to appear jerky on some monitors, or to be fuzzy and hard to see.

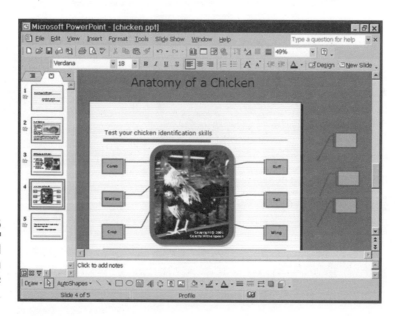

Figure B.6

Store unneeded presentation elements in the gray area.

PowerPoint handles a variety of image file created by a computer graphics program, scanned from photographs and drawings, downloaded from a clip art collection, or created with the PowerPoint drawing tools (such as lines, circles, and AutoShapes). If you insert image files that are not in standard Web formats (GIF and JPEG files), PowerPoint automatically converts them to GIF or JPEG when you save the presentation in a Web file format. When you add image files to the presentation, consider the file size. Larger files mean a longer download time and a greater chance that your audience will get bored waiting for the download (and possibly decide to go elsewhere instead of waiting). To reduce the size of images contained in the presentation, follow these steps:

1. Click on the Compress Pictures button on the Picture toolbar to open the Compress Pictures dialog box (shown in Figure B.7).

2. Click on the All Pictures in Document option button.

3. Click on the Web/Screen option button.

4. Place a checkmark in the Compress Pictures checkbox.

Figure B.7

Compress all the pictures in a presentation to help reduce the file size.

5. Place a checkmark in the Delete Cropped Areas of Pictures check-box.

6. Click on OK to open the Compress Pictures confirmation dialog box.

7. Click on Apply. The images in the Web presentation are reduced to 96 dpi.

The best sound file format to use in your Web-based presentation is the WAV file format, but you can also use MIDI, a widely used Web format. When using sound files in your Web-based presentation, keep in mind that PowerPoint only supports the playing of sound files in Internet Explorer 4.0 or later. If your audience uses an earlier version of Internet Explorer or any version of Netscape Navigator, the sounds will not play. Your audience also must have a soundcard and speakers attached to their computers to hear the sounds.

If you plan to use video files in the presentation, use the AVI or MPEG formats. In most instances, video files play either at full screen or at the size at which you inserted the video file on the slide and also start playing automatically. To give your audience control of the video file, insert the file as a Media Clip object (using the Insert, Object command). This adds play, pause, and stop controls to the video so your audience can watch and replay the video.

 NOTE To learn more about playing multimedia in PowerPoint presentations, visit **http://www.soniacoleman.com/Tutorials/PowerPoint/Multimedia.htm.**

Step 7: Preview Before You Publish

You might want an opportunity to see your Web site through your visitors' eyes. As you work on a site, take a look at the site in a Web browser. You don't need to publish the Web before you can open the browser and take a look. The easiest way to preview a site is to look at the individual pages from the Web Page Preview feature. This shows you what a visitor sees if they run the same version of Internet Explorer as is installed on your system, have the same size monitor, and use the same screen color and resolution settings. Here's how to test your site before you make it public:

1. Click on File, Web Page Preview to open the Web presentation in the default browser. The presentation in Figure B.8 displays in Internet Explorer 5.0 and uses the presentation outline as the navigation control. The presentation in Figure B.9 also displays in Internet Explorer 5.0 and uses hyperlinks and action buttons to navigate between slides.

2. Click on hyperlinks to see whether they lead to the correct pages.

3. Fix any problems in the presentation file, and preview the site again.

Figure B.8

To move from slide to slide, click on a hyperlink in the left frame.

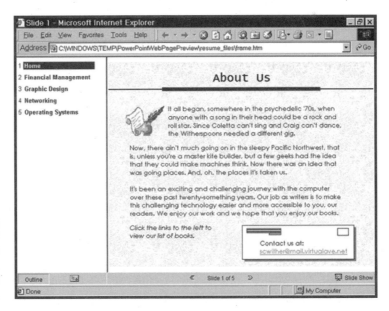

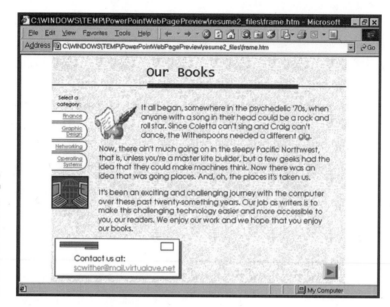

Figure B.9

Hyperlinks to the other slides in the presentation (found along the left edge of the slide) were created on the slide master.

TIP If you find that text does not display properly on a Web slide, make sure you have only one space between words, one space after each sentence, and no spaces at the end of the paragraph. Delete any extra spaces and preview the slides again.

Step 8: Save the Presentation as a Web Page

When you are satisfied with the way the presentation previews as a Web page, it's time to prepare the file for publishing. You have several options when saving PowerPoint presentations so they can be published to a Web site:

- Web page
- Web archive
- GIF files
- JPEG files

The most versatile method is to publish the presentation to a new (and empty) folder on your hard drive and to save it as a Web page. This method creates an HTML file and a supporting directory that you can easily upload to your Web host's server or add to a Web site created in FrontPage. For example, if the presentation is named pressie.ppt, the Web page version is called pressie.htm, and the supporting files are located in a folder named pressie_files. Here's how to create the Web presentation files:

1. Click on File, Save a Web Page to open the Save As dialog box (shown in Figure B.10).

2. Select the new folder on your computer to store the Web presentation files.

3. Type a name for the Web presentation in the File Name text box.

4. Click on the Change Title button to open the Set Page Title dialog box.

Figure B.10

Save the Web presentation files on your computer before you publish them to a Web server.

5. Type a title for the Web presentation in the Page Title text box. This title appears in the title bar of the browser when viewed over the Internet. Click on OK to return to the Save As dialog box.

6. Click on Save.

Step 9: Publish the Web Presentation

You have many ways to publish your presentation to a Web server, and you need to talk to your Web host to find out how. Your Web host might support any of the following publishing methods:

- FTP
- FrontPage
- Web folders

When using FTP or Web folders to publish the Web pages, you need to upload both the HTML file and the supporting folder. If you want to add the presentation to a FrontPage Web site, import the presentation and associated files into the FrontPage Web file and then create a hyperlink to the presentation HTML file. When your visitor clicks on the hyperlink, the presentation file appears and the visitor can browse the presentation just as they would any other Web page.

Step 10: Keep the Web Presentation Up-to-Date

After you publish your Web presentation, your job isn't over. It is important to keep current the information in the presentation. You might also find that you need to change or improve information and content. When you are ready to update your Web presentation, open the original presentation file (the one in the .ppt format) and make the changes. Then, go back to Step 9, resave the file in HTML format, and republish.

NOTE PowerPoint does not handle HTML files well. If you edit the HTML version of the presentation in PowerPoint, you might find the results not to your liking and they might not resemble the original presentation.

APPENDIX C

Online Resource Directory

As you work on your PowerPoint presentations, you might find some of these online sites to be of help. Some offer clip art or PowerPoint templates, others offer advice on graphics and presentation design, and still others provide resources for presentation equipment and slide generation.

Microsoft PowerPoint Sites

Microsoft provides several information and sample sites that help you use PowerPoint most effectively:

FAQ Page for Microsoft Newsgroups **(http://www.rdpslides.com/pptfaq/)**

A collection of frequently asked questions from the Microsoft PowerPoint newsgroup.

PowerPoint Newsgroup (point your newsgroup reader to **http://www.msnews.microsoft.com**, then the group Microsoft.public.powerpoint)

Visit the PowerPoint Newsgroup to discuss PowerPoint with fellow users.

PowerPoint Product Page **(http://officeupdate.microsoft.com/welcome/powerpoint.asp)**

This site includes document templates, PowerPoint help, updates, and resource kits.

Presentation-Oriented Web Sites

These sites are gathering spots for those interested in making presentations. On these sites, you'll find features that include articles, tips, and discussion areas where you can share presentation war stories:

Presentations.com **(http://www.presentations.com)**

This Web site is entirely about making presentations. You'll find information on new technology as well as tips about design and presentation.

Communications Media Management Association (CMMA) **(http://www.cmma.net)**

This is an association of managers of corporate and education media departments. The site provides some information on managing media services and current technology.

International Association of Presentation Professionals **(http://www.iapp.org)**

If you're thinking of turning pro after finishing this book, check this out.

Toastmasters International **(http://www.toastmasters.org)**

If you want to hone your personal presentation skills, check into this non-profit group that helps people with public speaking.

PowerPointers **(http://www.powerpointers.com)**

This site provides articles about public speaking and PowerPoint tips.

Great Speaking **(http://antion.com)**

This online magazine focuses on presentations, public speaking, and related information.

Presentation Equipment and Services

If you need a projector, printed handouts, or slides, you're likely to find help on one of these Web sites:

Go Slide City **(http://www.goslidecity.com)**

Send your PowerPoint presentation online to these people, and they'll ship 35mm slides on the same day.

ProjectorCentral.com **(http://www.projectorcentral.com)**

You can get information here on more than 1,000 projector models on this site that searches 2,000 dealers online.

ePresenter.com **(http://www.epresenter.com)**

Projectors, accessories, and presentation advice all appear on this site.

IQ Imaging **(http://iqimaging.com)**

This service converts PowerPoint presentations into 35mm slides.

Discount Projectors **(http://www.discountprojectors.com)**

If you want to get low-cost projection equipment, visit this site for prices and equipment information.

PrintBid.com **(http://www.printbid.com)**

When you need to print out handouts or supporting material for your presentations, this site can find you the best prices on printing services.

Data Translation **(http://www.b-way.com/videocapturecard)**

Data Translation's video capture and editing system is called Broadway. This site gives you a look at how to use it to add video to PowerPoint presentations.

Free Templates, Media Clips, and Plug-Ins

Here are some freebies: downloadable clip collections, demos and trial versions of plug-in software products, and various PowerPoint templates:

Microsoft Office Update Site **(http://officeupdate.Microsoft.com/)**

This site includes free PowerPoint templates as well as plug-ins and updates for PowerPoint.

Crystal Graphics **(http://www.crystalgraphics.com/weblink. 3d_sensations.main.html)**

Go here to get a 3-D plug-in for PowerPoint called Transitions. This plug-in adds television-quality 3-D effects to your slides. You can get a downloadable trial version and even some free effects here.

A Bit Better Corporation **(http://www.bitbetter.com)**

A Bit Better offers a collection of Screen Beans clip art. PowerPoint comes with several of those little stick figure creatures, but if you need more, this is the place to go.

Clip Media for Sale

The following companies sell clip media collections:

Artbeats (**http://www.artbeats.com**)

Dynamic Graphics (**http://www.dgusa.com**)

Animated Communications (**http://www.3dchor.com**)

Digital Juice (**http://www.digitaljuice.com**)

Dazzle Multimedia, Inc. (**http://www.dazzle.com**)

OGM Production Music (**http://www.ogmmusic.com**)

Sound Ideas (**http://www.sound-ideas.com**)

Design Resources Online

Although creating PowerPoint presentations isn't exactly graphic design or exactly Web design, it does call on you to use design methods and principles from each area. Sometimes to get ideas for use of color, graphics, and the balance of words and images on a page, it's helpful to visit design Web sites. Here are a handful that you can turn to when you need inspiration or advice.

Print Magazine (**http://www.printmag.com**)

How Design Magazine (**http://www.howdesign.com**)

Creative Business (**http://www.creativebusiness.com**)

DesignBoom (**http://www.designboom.com**)

Identifont (**http://www.identifont.com**)

American Center for Design (**http://www.ac4d.org**)

Corporate Design Foundation (**http://www.cdf.org**)

Resources for Writing and Research

You can have all the clip art and colors in the universe, but the foundation of your presentation is still the words you use to get your message across. For help researching and writing your presentation content, try some of these useful sites:

CIA World Factbook (**http://www.odci.gov/cia/publications/factbook**)

Information Please Almanac (**http://www.infoplease.com**)

Acronym Finder (**http://www.acronymfinder.com**)

Encyberpedia Dictionary and Glossary (**http://www.encyberpedia.com/glossary.htm**)

Roget's Internet Thesaurus (**http://www.thesaurus.com/**)

Encarta Online (**http://Encarta.msn.com**)

The Internet Public Library (**http://www.ipl.org**)

UseIt.com articles on design (**http://www.useit.com/alertbox/9710a.html**)

Online English Grammar (**http://www.edunet.com/English/grammar/index.html**)

Yale Web Style Guide **(http://info.med.yale.edu/caim/manual/index.html)**

Famous Firsts **(http://www.corsinet.com/trivia/1-triv.html)**

Bartlett's Familiar Quotations **(http://www.bartleby.com/)**

APPENDIX D

Talk the Talk with Speech Recognition

Ever wanted to tell your computer off? With this version of Power-Point, which supports a limited version of speech recognition, you can—or at least you can enter text and tell it to execute some basic commands just by speaking.

Speech recognition support built into Office XP allows you to interact with your computer through speech in several ways; you can:

239

⚙ Say text and PowerPoint will enter it on your slides

⚙ Speak the names of commands to activate a tool function

⚙ Speak common keyboard functions such as Enter, Tab, Escape, and so on and your computer will execute them

⚙ Enter some keyboard characters into a document by speaking their names

NOTE Before you can use the speech recognition feature, you have to install it, because it isn't installed during the typical product installation for Office.

Is speech recognition going to leave your hands free for using the stereo remote control or playing solitaire while you work? Hardly. But it's an interesting feature to play around with and may save you a bit of time. And learning to use it now will lay the groundwork for more sophisticated speech interface capabilities that surely lay somewhere down Microsoft's Yellow Brick Road.

What You Need to Speak to Your Computer

You didn't just come into the world understanding language, and your computer didn't either. You have to do a few things to get it ready to pay attention to your spoken word. First, you need a high-quality soundcard, a microphone, and headset. Your best bet is to get what's called a close-talk headset; that is, a headset with a microphone incorporated into it. This cuts down on outside noise that might interfere when speaking to a microphone built into your computer, for example. Finally, you need to activate the speech recognition feature from the Tools menu of Word 2002.

TIP

■ ■

Will speech recognition slow down your computer? It could. That's why Microsoft requires that you have a computer with at least a 400MHz processor speed and 128MB of RAM. If you've got less computer than that, you'll have to leave speech recognition alone till you upgrade your system.

■ ■

Installing Speech Recognition

To activate speech recognition in Office XP, first you have to install it. First put the Office XP software in your CD drive, and then follow these steps to install the speech feature:

1. Select Start, Control Panel.

2. In the Control Panel, click on Add/Remove Programs. The Add/Remove Programs Properties dialog box, shown in Figure D.1, appears.

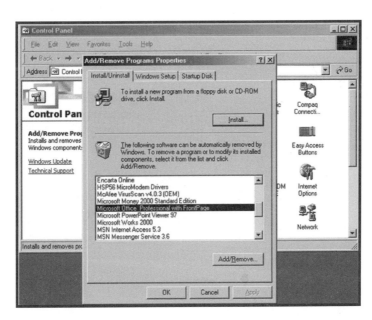

Figure D.1

Here's where you can install a new program, or add components of an already-installed program.

3. Scroll down and locate Microsoft Office Professional with Front-Page and click to select it.

4. Click on Add/Remove.

5. In the Setup dialog that appears next, select the Specific Features option and click Next. Another Setup dialog box appears, with a list of possible features to install.

6. Click on the plus sign next to the Office Shared Features item. A list of Office Shared features opens.

7. Click on the plus sign next to the Alternative User input item; it opens showing two choices, Speech and Handwriting, as shown in Figure D.2.

8. Click on the Speech item in the list, and click the Update button. Windows installs the Speech feature.

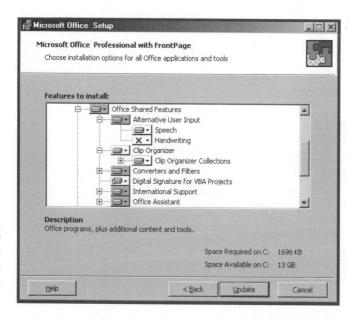

Figure D.2

Various features are nested in an outline format in this dialog box.

Activating Speech Recognition

In order to begin using speech recognition, you have to activate the feature, and go through an approximately 15 minute training session. During this session you will set your microphone levels, and let Office learn something about your voice patterns and pronunciation by reading text into your microphone.

Microsoft suggests that you activate Office Speech Recognition the first time in Word. Follow these steps:

1. Open Word 2002 (Start, Programs, Microsoft Word 2002).

2. Select Tools, Speech. The Speech dialog box shown in Figure D.3 appears.

3. Click Next to begin the wizard. The Microphone Wizard Welcome screen, shown in Figure D.4 appears. It's important to read through each of the screens in this wizard, because they provide advice about sound settings for your computer and how to use speech recognition.

4. Make sure your microphone and speakers are connected to your computer, and then adjust your headset to match the illustration in this dialog box.

5. Click Next to continue. The Test Microphone dialog box appears.

6. Read the sentence in quotes. As you do, the wizard checks your microphone and its volume. You'll see small lines on the monitor as you read, indicating that your microphone is working, as shown in Figure D.5.

Figure D.3

This Welcome dialog box tells you what you'll encounter as you work through the speech recognition activation process.

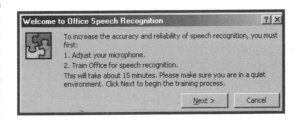

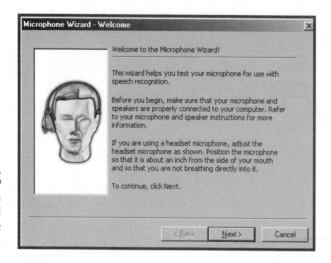

Figure D.4

You can learn about suggested microphone settings here.

7. Make adjustments to your microphone setup in Windows or your speaking volume until the volume meter shows that it's receiving sound.

8. Click on Next to proceed. The Test Positioning dialog box shown in Figure D.6 appears.

9. Read the sentence in quotes. The wizard plays this back to you. Note whether the recording is clear or breathy.

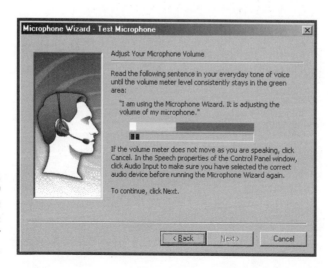

Figure D.5

As you read, the monitor shows the volume of your microphone.

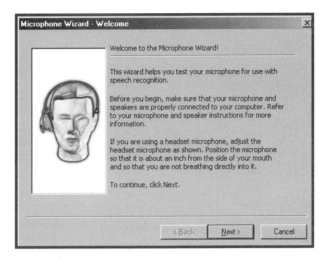

Figure D.6

If your microphone isn't positioned properly, it can result in breathiness which can distort your voice.

10. If the playback isn't clear, adjust your headset or hand microphone and read the sentence again, until it is clear.

11. Click on Finish when you're satisfied with the recording quality. The Default Speech Profile dialog box shown in Figure D.7 appears.

Figure D.7

This dialog box is the beginning of your training process.

12. This dialog box is the start of the speech training process, where Office Speech Recognition learns your speech patterns. Be sure that you are in a quiet environment (turn off that rap music and shut the door) so the training process that you're about to go through has the best chance of succeeding.

13. Click Next to begin. The next dialog box, shown in Figure D.8, offers a few settings to you.

14. Click the appropriate radio button to indicate your gender and age group. This helps Office anticipate the general characteristics of your voice.

15. Click Next to proceed. The next Speech Profile dialog box appears, as shown in Figure D.9.

16. Read this dialog box; it provides advice about how to read sample sentences for the best results in training speech recognition. If you want to hear an example of how to read, click the Sample button.

17. When you're ready to begin reading, click Next.

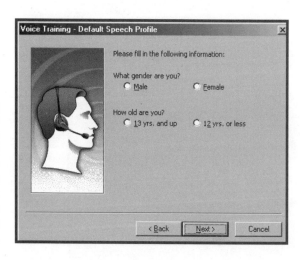

Figure D.8

Office wants to know something about the person who will be speaking, which it does by asking you to make selections here.

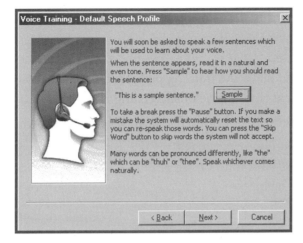

Figure D.9

Office provides a sample of how to read sentences in this dialog box.

Training Speech Recognition

You are now at the beginning portion of the setup that involves training the speech feature to recognize and understand your speech patterns. You will see a series of screens like the one in Figure D.10 that provide text for you to read. It's important that you speak as clearly as you can into your microphone. If you wish to pause the recording, click on the Pause button. When you've finished reading one screen, click Next to proceed to the next.

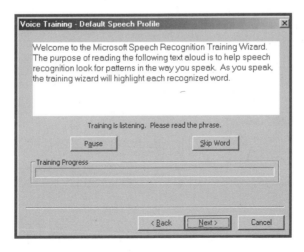

Figure D.10

If you want to pause the reading, click the Pause button located here.

As you read, words will be highlighted as they are recognized by the program, as shown in Figure D.11. If you reach a point where the highlighting stops, that means that Office can't understand the word. First repeat it as clearly as you can; if it still doesn't highlight, click the Skip Word button. The problem word will be highlighted and you can continue reading from the next unhighlighted word.

When you have completed reading all the screens, Office will open a video training session on the speech feature; the opening screen of this is shown in Figure D.12.

When the training demo is over, the Language toolbar will appear. Close Word, and open PowerPoint. The Language toolbar will still be available there, as shown in Figure D.13. Now you're ready to begin using the speech feature.

TIP

If you run through the Training session again from time to time, it helps Office get better at recognizing your voice patterns.

Figure D.11

Sometimes you can't get Office to understand a word you say; when that happens, repeat it as clearly as possible.

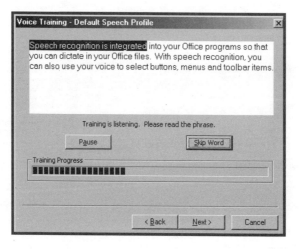

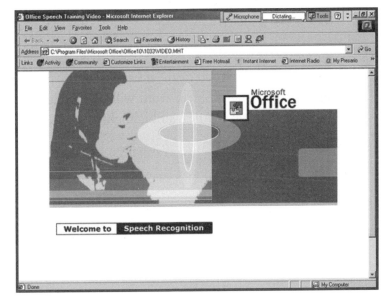

Figure D.12

This sequence walks you through the basics of using Office Speech Recognition.

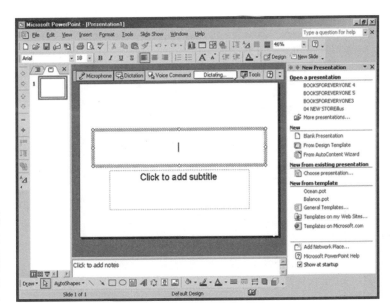

Figure D.13

This is a floating toolbar; you can move it around your screen as you like.

Entering Text By Speech

The Language toolbar, which you display at any time by selecting Tools, Speech, allows you to toggle between two modes: Dictation and Voice Command. Dictation allows you to speak text and it will be entered in the selected area of PowerPoint (for example, in the title placeholder for a slide). Voice Command mode allows you to speak commands, such as Backspace, and the command will be initiated.

Entering text with Office Speech Recognition is both simple, and difficult. It's simple because all you do to get going is click on the Dictation tool and begin speaking. It's difficult because the speech feature isn't yet sophisticated enough to recognize everything you say. In Figure D.14, for example, I said "Annual sales review for the Acme Corporation". PowerPoint entered "Annual sales review to the took me or Parisian," as shown in Figure D.14.

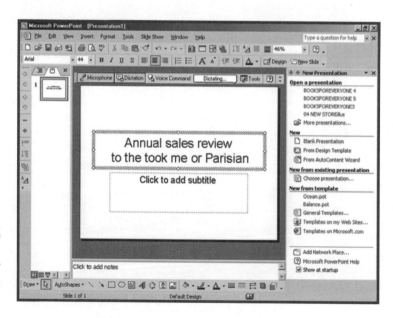

Figure D.14

"Acme Corporation" came out as "or Parisian" with the speech feature.

You can stop at any point and make corrections with your keyboard and mouse. In fact, you're likely to have to go back through everything entered with Speech Recognition to make sure it understood what you said, and to correct things like capitalizations of titles in slides and proper names.

Giving Hands Off Commands

In addition to entering text with the speech feature, you can give several voice commands by speaking them. You can select these from Table D.1.

You can also select text and speak toolbar commands. For example, if you select text and, in Voice Command mode, say "Font", the font list on the Formatting toolbar opens, as shown in Figure D.15.

Getting this and other features of Office Speech Recognition to work smoothly is a matter of practice and patience. If you like the feature, you can use it in every Office program. But remember, as with any new technology, it takes some investment to reap the rewards

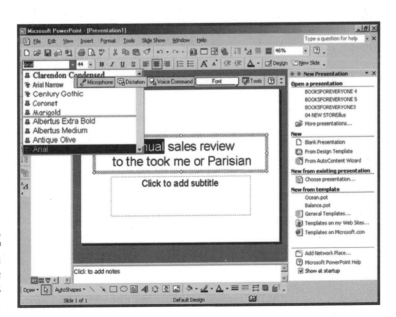

Figure D.15

Simply speaking a tool button name activates its function.

TABLE D.1 OFFICE XP SPEECH RECOGNITION COMMANDS

What You Say	What's Inserted in Your Document	What You Say	What's Inserted in Your Document
Ampersand	&	New line	Enter
Asterisk	*	New paragraph	Enter twice
At sign, at	@	Open brace	{
Backslash	\	Open bracket	[
Caret	^	Paren	(
Close brace	}	Percent, percent sign	%
Close Paren	)	Period, dot	.
Colon	:	Plus, plus sign	+
Comma	,	Pound sign	#
Dollar sign	$	Question mark	?
Double dash	--	Quote, open quote	"
Ellipsis	...	Right bracket	]
End quote, Close quote	"	Semicolon	;
Equals	=	Single quote	'
Exclamation point	!	Slash	/
Greater than	>	Tilde	~
Hyphen, dash	-	Underscore	_
Less than	<	Vertical bar		

Glossary

3-D style—A tool on the Drawing toolbar. A setting for 3-D effects on text or objects.

Action buttons—Clickable icons accessed from the Drawing toolbar that you can place on a PowerPoint slide. When a user clicks on an action button during a slide-show presentation, the program performs a specified action, such as display the first slide in the presentation or play a sound file.

Alignment—Placement of a text object or other object on a slide in relationship to the outside edges of the slide or the border of a placeholder. Standard alignment settings are Align Left, Center, Justify, and Align Right.

Animation scheme—Preset animation sequences that affect the style of transition used when changing from one slide to another during a PowerPoint slide show, or to reveal or hide objects in a sequence once a new slide is displayed.

AutoContent—Presentation content templates that are based on the type of presentation a user is creating and that contain placeholder slide content.

AutoContent Wizard—A series of dialog boxes; based on the user input in these dialog boxes, this wizard generates a presentation with AutoContent.

AutoCorrect—A feature of PowerPoint that automatically corrects certain common input mistakes, such as commonly misspelled words or capitalization errors; also generates common symbols, such as a trademark ™, from regular text entries.

AutoFit— A feature of AutoCorrect, the AutoFit feature automatically resizes text in a text placeholder to fit. An AutoFit tool appears on your slide the first time AutoFit resizes text in a text object, providing options for adjusting the fit of text within a placeholder.

AutoFormat—A feature of PowerPoint that makes certain automatic formatting changes to the appearance of text in a presentation, such as highlighting hyperlinks. You can turn off the AutoFormat feature in the AutoCorrect Options dialog box.

AutoShape—Pre-designed drawing tools that allow you to draw a variety of shapes, such as block arrows, stars and banners, and flowcharts.

Background—The color or pattern that fills a slide behind any text or graphic objects.

Callout—A combination text-and-line element that uses a style of line to point to and label an element on a slide.

Clip art—Pre-designed line drawings, photos, sound files, or video clips provided with PowerPoint that you can insert on any PowerPoint slide.

Collapse—To hide detail levels of an outline and display only higher-level headings (in the Outline tab of the Normal view).

Color scheme—Preset color combinations you can apply to slides that affect the colors of the background, title, and bullet text.

Comments—Notes that you can attach to individual slides. You can use comments when working with others on a group presentation to share background information. Comments are not visible while presenting a slide show.

Connector—A drawing object; a line connecting two end points.

Content layouts—Slide layouts that determine the placement of a non-text object placeholder; from this placeholder you can generate several types of content, such as graphics, tables, and charts, on a slide.

Demote—To move an item in an outline to a lower level of detail in the outline.

Design template—A set of design elements you can apply to slides, including text formatting, graphic elements, and background settings.

Discussion—Also called Web discussions. The Web Discussion feature allows you to place comments on a Web page or a browser-viewable document. These comments are displayed along with the document, but they are actually saved on the server hosting the discussion.

Expand—To open an entire outline so that all levels of headings are displayed (on the Outline tab of Normal view).

Fill color—The color chosen to fill the inside of a drawing object, such as a rectangle.

Filter (Discussion)—A feature in Web discussions that allows you to filter out comments using certain criteria. Using a filter, you can view comments made only by certain individuals, for example.

Flowchart—A type of AutoShape drawing object that uses lines and boxes to show the progression of a process.

Grayscale—A display without color, using only black, white, and shades of gray. You can use settings in PowerPoint to display only grayscale images onscreen or print slides using grayscale.

Grid—A pattern of intersecting horizontal and vertical points that you can display on a PowerPoint slide; grids are useful in lining up objects on a slide more accurately.

Group—A feature of the PowerPoint Drawing menu that allows you to assemble separate objects into one group so you can move them or resize them all with one action.

Guides—A set of horizontal and vertical intersecting lines that mark the middle of a slide. You can use guides to align objects on a slide more accurately. Guides can be moved anywhere on a slide and multiple sets of guides can be created by placing your mouse over a guide and pressing Ctrl+ the right mouse button and dragging an additional guide to a new location.

Handouts—Printed versions of slides in a presentation. You can print various configurations of handouts, such as six slides to a page or a single slide to a page.

HTML—Hypertext Markup Language, the language used to create Web pages. In PowerPoint, you can save slides in HTML format for use on the Web.

Hyperlink—A way to instantly display a Web page, files, or a slide in a PowerPoint document. Clicking on a hyperlink in PowerPoint can take you to a Web page, a document file, or another slide in your presentation.

Indent—To move a heading in an outline to a more detailed level in the outline.

Line Style—Settings you can apply to lines on a slide that control their thickness, or apply one of several dashed line styles.

Link—*See* Hyperlink.

Macro—A series of user-input keystrokes or programming commands that result in an action; this program sequence can be recorded, saved, and replayed with a menu command.

Master—A PowerPoint element where all details of a design template and other objects are kept and applied to all the slides in a presentation, or a set of slides. It is possible to have several sets of masters for any single presentation. You can override master settings on individual slides and apply different settings to slides, handouts, and notes.

Meeting Minder—A feature accessed through the Tool menu that allows you to schedule meetings among teams collaborating on a PowerPoint presentation and keep notes from the meeting.

Narration—A sound file of commentary that you can record to be played back with a slide show.

Normal View—The view in PowerPoint where you edit either individual slides or the presentation outline.

Nudge—A feature used to move objects around a slide in small increments.

Object—Any text, graphic, sound, or drawing item. Even though it can contain several text characters or graphic elements, an object can be moved, resized, and formatted as one element.

Office Clipboard—A pane you can display in PowerPoint that allows you to cut and paste text or objects for use on any slide in your presentation, or in other programs.

Online broadcast—To present a PowerPoint slide show in HTML format over a network using Microsoft Outlook or another email program to schedule and notify participants. Live broadcasts can be accompanied by audio and video if the presenter and viewers have the proper equipment.

Online collaboration—A set of tools for creating a PowerPoint presentation when you're working with a group. You use collaboration tools to schedule and run online meetings or discussions.

Outline—An organizational scheme where you place headings at indented levels based on their level of detail in a presentation; these levels can also reflect the relative importance of a particular idea or topic in an overall presentation.

Output—The medium you intend to use to present a slide show, such as printed handouts, traditional slides, an HTML file on the Web, and so on.

Pen Color—In a slide show, the color you select for the pen tool you can use to draw or write on a slide during a presentation.

Placeholder—A preset element you can use to easily insert specific text or objects on a slide.

Pointer—A feature of slide shows that allows you to point to items onscreen or select a pen tool to write or draw on slides during a presentation.

Print preview—A display of PowerPoint slides in a presentation as they would appear in printed form using WYSIWYG (what you see is what you get) format.

Promote—To move a heading to a higher level in an outline.

Reviewer—A person who views a PowerPoint presentation and places comments in it. Using the Review function, you can combine different reviewers' comments into one document.

Revisions task pane—A window the originator of a review presentation can display that itemizes the changes made to slides by all reviewers.

Rotate—A tool that allows you to turn an object up to 359 degrees to change its orientation on a page.

Shadow style—Settings for the style of shadow effect you can apply to an object.

Slide design—Design templates you can use to automatically apply a background, text formatting, and graphic objects to slides in a presentation.

Slide layout—Preset arrangements of text and object placeholders on a slide.

Slide master—A PowerPoint element where all details of a design template and other objects are kept and applied to all the slides or a set of slides within a presentation. You can override master settings on individual slides.

Slide show—The presentation mode in PowerPoint.

Slide Sorter—A view where all slides in a presentation appear in thumbnail versions in the order in which they will appear in the slide show. Slide Sorter View is useful for copying, deleting, and reorganizing slides.

Slide transition—An effect used when moving from one slide to another in a slide show.

Speaker's notes—Notes you can store in a presentation that appear next to slides in a printed handout to help a presenter remember relevant details.

Speech recognition—A technology that enables software such as a word processor or PowerPoint to perform a command or record the text spoken by a computer user.

Spin button—A form button that allows a user to change a setting by clicking either of a set of arrows.

Summary slide—A slide that contains titles of other slides in a presentation.

Task pane—An onscreen area in PowerPoint that displays features and tools related to a common activity.

Team Site—A PowerPoint collaboration feature; you can create a Team Site based on a FrontPage template as a Web location for exchanging documents, holding discussions, and posting announcements. A Team Site must be hosted on a server with Microsoft SharePoint installed.

Text layouts—Slide layouts with pre-positioned text objects such as a title, subtitle, or bullet list.

Text wrapping—A feature that automatically wraps text down to the beginning of the next line when the edge of a margin or placeholder is reached.

Timings—Settings you can make to control the playback timing of a slide show presentation.

Title slide—A slide layout containing both title and subtitle placeholders.

Voice command—A software command given by speaking, when using speech-recognition software.

Web discussions—A feature that allows you to place comments on a Web page or a browser-viewable document. These comments are displayed along with the document, but they are actually saved on a discussion server.

Web page preview—A feature allowing you to see how a PowerPoint presentation will appear when displayed on the Web.

WordArt—An applet included as a shared application in Office XP and accessible from the PowerPoint Drawing toolbar that allows you to add special formatting effects to text.

INDEX

License Agreement/Notice of Limited Warranty